# An Introduction to the Prose Poem

Edited by Brian Clements
and Jamey Dunham

Firewheel Editions

Firewheel Editions
Box 7
Western Connecticut State University
181 White St.
Danbury, CT 06810

http://firewheel-editions.org
info@firewheel-editions.org

ISBN-10: 0966575474
ISBN-13: 9780966575477

The editors would like to thank: Eileen Dorcey for her assistance in the preparation of this book; Fred Courtright of The Permissions Company for his assistance in acquiring reprint permissions; and Western Connecticut State University for the CSU/AAUP Research Grant that helped to make this book possible.

Cover art and design by Thomas Nackid, www.tomnackidart.com

firewheel
editions

## Also from Firewheel Editions

*Sentence: A Journal of Prose Poetics*
*Mille et un sentiments*, by Denise Duhamel
*Trompe l'Oeil*, by Kristin Ryling
*The Future Called Something O'Clock*, by Daniel Luévano

Forthcoming:
*Hands of Antiquity*, by Edward Bartók-Baratta
*Had Slaves*, by Catherine Sasanov
*The important thing is…*, by Marjorie Tesser
*The Book of Willie (Revised Standard Version)*, by Charles Kesler
*Help (in 47 Languages)*, by Denise Duhamel

## Also from Brian Clements

*And How to End It*, Quale Press
*Disappointed Psalms*, Meritage Press
*Essays Against Ruin*, Texas Review Press

## Also from Jamey Dunham

*The Bible of Lost Pets*, Salt Modern Poets

# Table of Contents

## Preface

The idea of "prose poetry" has been around in various incarnations since at least February of 1831, when the term appeared in a British magazine's exuberant paean to the possibilities of poetic prose[1] years before anyone actually set out to write pieces self-consciously conceived as "prose poems." Yet, even after a few fits of popularity during the 20th century, the prose poem has come into wide acceptance in the U.S. only recently. Within the last 15 years the prose poem began appearing commonly in mainstream literary journals and providing the subject of several anthologies such as this one. Why first the resistance, and why then the new-found popularity of the prose poem?

The resistance may have to do with the name itself—many readers new to the prose poem wonder "How can there be such a thing as a prose poem? Isn't that an oxymoron?" But, not unlike "free verse," the oxymoronic name captures the complex nature of a beast bred to challenge conventional assumptions about what poetry is and what it can do.

While many of us think of poems as always consisting of verse (whether "free" or not), the fact is that many traditions of poetic prose around the world—such as the Japanese haibun, the Chinese fu, texts adapted from the oral traditions of many indigenous people, and some passages from the King James Version of the Bible and other religious texts—are precursors and models for what, especially since the publication of Charles Baudelaire's *Paris Spleen: Petits Poèmes en Prose* in 1862, has been known variously as the poem in prose, the proeme, or the prose poem.

---

[1] See *Such Rare Citings: The Prose Poem in English Literature*, N. Santilli. Madison, NJ: Fairleigh Dickinson, 2002.

A Brief History

In 1842, a collection of short prose vignettes by Aloysius Bertrand, *Gaspard de la nuit*, appeared in print. These short poetic narratives and meditations were highly influential on Baudelaire's composition of his *Petites Poèmes en Prose;* Baudelaire's innovation, in turn, reflected in the work of young Arthur Rimbaud, a French poet whose short life yielded a wealth of prose poems now considered classics of the genre. Baudelaire's use of the term "poème en prose" and the high degree of success of these writers working in French have led many to think of the prose poem as an essentially French genre. This habit is supported by the further evolution of the genre in the work of Mallarmé and subsequently the Surrealists and other early 20th Century authors composing in French. Poets such as Francis Ponge, Max Jacob, and Henri Micheaux were among the poets working in French who adopted the prose poem as a tool useful to them in their quest for imaginative liberation.

During the literary explosion of the Modernist period, many poets working in Spanish—such as Nobel Laureates Pablo Neruda, Gabriella Mistral, and Vicente Alexaindre—adopted the prose poem as an expansive tool that allowed them to incorporate narrative and free-form meditation into the poem without sacrificing the lyricism that so many of them adored.

Until the 1960's and 1970's and the resurgence of interest in internationalist studies in the United States, the prose poem was considered stereotypically the territory of French- and Spanish-language poets; but in fact poets were working in the prose poem all over Europe: in German (Bertolt Brecht), English (Gertrude Stein), Greek (George Seferis), and Polish (Czeslaw Milosz and Zbigniew Herbert), to name only a few examples.

The prose poem underwent a renaissance in the U.S. in the 60's and 70's in the hands of poets such as Robert Bly, James Wright, and W. S. Merwin, who wrote prose poems themselves but perhaps more importantly translated the work of the great European and South American prose poets into English. The visibility of the prose poem was promoted by the work of Russell Edson, James Tate, and Charles Simic. By the end of the 70's the prose poem had caught on as a fairly fashionable mode of writing for American poets. In 1976, the prose poet Michael Benedikt edited the first major anthology of prose poems, *The Prose Poem: An International Anthology*, gathering work from around the world. Benedikt's anthology established a history and a tradition for the prose poem, which has only grown in popularity since. Today, most literary journals in the U.S. publish prose poems alongside verse, free verse, literary nonfiction, and prose fiction.

## Defining the Prose Poem

The simplest definition is that a prose poem is a poem written in prose. As Michael Benedikt points out in his introduction to *The Prose Poem: An International Anthology*, the prose poem can make use of every poetic device that one can find in verse with the exception of the line break. Some readers who subscribe to the conservative idea that verse is a necessary component of poetry will have trouble with this idea. Readers, however, who are willing to include in their concepts of poetry the concrete poem, slam poetry, performance poetry, visual poetry, and other varieties of poetic composition will have no problem at all conceding that a poem can be composed of prose. It is not the format of the work that determines whether it is a poem. In fact, when a free verse poem of complicated structure is read out loud—or even some verse poems—most listeners would have trouble discerning the line structure. In verse, the point of the line is to build rhythm and music in order to enhance the meaning or effect of the poem; this end can be achieved in the prose sentence as well.

The prose poem is no less equipped than verse, then, to build rhythm and music, to produce meaning, or to affect a reader. The prose poem does present one significant challenge, though, in that it does not have the line ending to use as a tool in achieving those goals. In verse or free verse, the tension between line structure and sentence structure is an important machine for the generation of pace, rhythm, and, sometimes, meaning. In the prose poem, pace and rhythm must be built entirely within the sentence itself and in the play among sentences. It is incumbent upon the prose poet to find another way to generate tension within the poem—this substitution is frequently achieved via surrealistic anti-logic, bizarre narrative, lushness of language, innovative structure, or experiments with grammar and syntax.

## Prose Poem: Form or Genre?

It is important to remember that most of the texts that we refer to as prose poems were conceived by their authors as *poems* that just happen to be written in prose, perhaps because the author saw the prose poem as the best tool to achieve the end desired. In that sense, we can say that all prose poems are poems, just as all sonnets are poems, and that comparison might lead us to think that the prose poem is a form.

However, whereas all true sonnets are composed of 14 lines, are written in iambic pentameter, and follow one of several basic rhyme schemes, there are no "rules" for the prose poem; the only requirements are that it be written in prose and be presented in the context of poetry. In that sense, one might argue that whether or not a text is a prose poem is, beyond those two stipulations, entirely a matter of *context*—a combination of *intent* on the part of the author, *perception* on the part of the reader, and an environment (say a book of poems, a literary journal, or a poetry reading), that encourages intent and perception to meet.

While some critics have posited that brevity is a requirement of the prose poem, poets such as John Ashbery, William Carlos Williams, and Robert Creeley have written prose poems up to full book length as well as long sequences of prose poems.

For these reasons, it is perhaps best to think of the prose poem as a sub-genre of poetry rather than as a form.

## Distinguishing Prose Poems from Other Short Prose

This is where we encounter difficulty. No one has yet created a definition of "poetry" that fits all cases and excludes all other genres. So it is difficult to determine in the abstract the genre of a text that sits on perceived boundaries of poem/story or poem/essay. Inability to define, though, does not preclude ability to differentiate. Many types of very short fiction (sometimes called microfiction, sudden fiction, flash fiction) such as in the work of Donald Barthelme or Yasunari Kawabata are difficult if not impossible to distinguish from prose poems; as David Lehman, editor of *Great American Prose Poems,* argues, these texts may be both short fiction and prose poems, or they may be something else entirely. However, when the term "short short story" is used we can make a differentiation.

Here our idea that the prose poem is a sub-genre of the poem comes in handy. If there is any practical difference between a prose poem and the short short story, the difference must derive from the fact that a prose poem is a poem and short short stories are a variety of short story. Prose poems may or may not be fictional, but short short stories, if the term is to have any meaning, must refer to very short examples of the "short story" genre; in Western literature the term implies a character-driven piece of fiction in which a change occurs in the character (who may also be the narrator) over the duration of the action. Because the short short story is so specific, we can differentiate between it and the prose poem—but it's more difficult to state a meaningful difference between some prose poems and some instances of microfiction or flash fiction that do not participate in the conventions of the short short story.

## Varieties of Prose Poetry

Critic Michel Delville argues that there may be as many kinds of prose poems as there are practitioners of the prose poem. But there are a number of common strategies of composition that prose poets have used repeatedly—the list poem, the epistolary poem, the object poem, the aphorism, for example. Because prose poems have no intrinsic "form" of their own, they frequently seek out other cultural forms as a kind of template or for a set of conventions within which to elaborate a structure. This anthology describes a number of commonly used strategies and provides examples of those strategies at work.

Though the prose poem is not a "form" and it has no formal requirements, it would be a mistake to assume that prose poems have no *structure*. In fact, structure in the prose poem is the revelation of the poem's meanings, and one convenient way to talk about structure in prose poems is to talk about their *strategies*. We do no want to suggest, though, that these strategies are static types into which all prose poems can or must fit—they are simply categories that identify common tendencies, that make discussion of the poems simpler, and that might provide prose poem beginners with models for their own poems.

Nor is an individual prose poem necessarily restricted to one of our categories. Many of the prose poems in this book could fit into two or even more categories; one could also create additional categories that include poems we've placed elsewhere in the book—an Ekphrastic Prose Poem section, for example, might include the prose poems by George Kalamaras, R. L. Rimas, and

Jeff Davis, or a Political Prose Poem section that might include the prose poems by Andrew Neuendorf, Carolyn Forché, Brian Clements, and others. In short, this book is about identifying some *possibilities* of the prose poem, not about confining the prose poem to a certain range of expression.

## Where to Find Prose Poems

Since 2002, several new journals have appeared that are devoted to prose poem traditions—*Sentence: A Journal of Prose Poetics*, *Double Room*, and *CUE* are vital indicators of the health of the prose poem. Most contemporary literary journals in the U.S. and Great Britain (including *American Poetry Review, Fence, Quarter After Eight, jubilat, Agni,* and many others) and many journals in Europe and South America publish prose poems regularly; some have even published special prose poetry issues. Many new anthologies have appeared in the last several years, including *Great American Prose Poems, Models of the Universe, The Party Train, No Boundaries, Freedom to Breathe, The Best of The Prose Poem: An International Journal, Bear Flag Republic, The House of Your Dream,* and *The PP/FF Anthology*.

Other Useful Books about Prose Poetry


Delville, Michel. *The American Prose Poem: Poetic Form and the Boundaries of Genre.* Gainesville: University Press of Florida, 1998.

Fredman, Stephen. *Poet's Prose: The Crisis in American Verse.* 2nd ed. Cambridge: Cambridge University Press, 1990.

Monroe, Jonathan. *A Poverty of Objects: The Prose Poem and the Politics of Genre.* Ithaca: Cornell University Press, 1987.

Monte, Steven. *Invisible Fences: Prose Poetry as a Genre in French and American Literature.* Lincoln: University of Nebraska Press, 2000.

Murphy, Marguerite S. *A Tradition of Subversion: The Prose Poem in English from Wilde to Ashbery.* Amherst: University of Massachusetts Press, 1992.

Santilli, N. Such Rare Citings: *The Prose Poem in English Literature.* Madison, NJ: Fairleigh Dickinson, 2002.

# Anecdote

An anecdote is a brief narrative account based upon a personal experience or set in a historically recognizable context. It differs from strategies such as the fable primarily in its factual tone and circumstance, though some poets have used the conventions of anecdote in fictitious work.

The central purpose of the anecdote usually has less to do with outlining a moral than with stating a truth or insight brought to light by the events of the story. Our usage of the word *anecdote* is derived from the title of a biography by Procopius of the Roman emperor Justinian I, *Anecdota*, which is usually translated as *Secret History*; that fact may help to explain the strong biographical element in anecdote as it is most commonly used today.

The tendency toward the autobiographical/historical account is evident in many of our selections here, though the individual poets vary the premises and outcomes. Whereas the poems by Daryl Scroggins, Kenneth Koch, and Peter Johnson take a somewhat informal and sometimes humorous approach, Pablo Neruda's "Ceremony" remains objective to the point of stoicism as it relays an account from a superstitious sea voyage. Carolyn Forché's "The Colonel" relates its story with a combination of matter-of-factness and authenticity ("What you have heard is true") that culminates in a chilling final image. John Martone's "Ghost Money" and Ana Delgadillo's "Surrounding My Birth in Veracruz," while based on personal experience and factual details, acquire from their atmospheres a mythic or fabulist sensibility.

All of the poems here, though, transcend the individual event on which the poem is premised to arrive if not at an epiphany then at least at a powerful portrait that resonates far beyond the significance of the initial experience itself. Mark Halperin's "Buying a Dictionary" derives simple pleasure from simple events;

in their stark realism, Sean Mclain Brown's "tagmemics" and Cecilia Woloch's "My Mother's Birds" uncover hard-won truths from hard-lived facts. As in James Wright's "Honey," where the speaker begins the poem by recalling the deathbed parting of his own father, the recollected anecdotes in these poems help the speaker and the reader to arrive at a fuller view of the events, of the world in which the events occurred, and sometimes of themselves.

## John Martone

### Ghost Money

In Ho Chi Minh City one morning at the end, wandering streets and collecting souvenirs of trash—pottery shards, broken toys, anything that might help later—I come on a trail of ghost money and begin picking up every scrap. As this is a morning of many funerals, I'm a millionaire soon enough, wandering through two districts, pockets full, and my plastic grocery bag as well. Strangers laugh and flee. Then, lost for hours, I can't find my room or street with its families living under tarps. It takes me till noon to find my way back, but the woman who sold me my daily bowl of vegetarian soup and almond cookies isn't worried at all when I offer a wad of soiled bills.

Later, a horrified friend says, if I want ghost money, I should buy it at a shop, not get it out of the street. What kind of Buddhist would do such a thing! The spirits will feel cheated, go hungry, surely pursue me. He is plenty serious, and I suddenly realize just who I am. Tonight I retrace my path for hours again, dropping money in the street as inconspicuously as possible, until every bill's gone. Gone beyond. My pockets and plastic bag hold only scraps of schoolbook jottings, empty towelette wrappers, crumpled cigarette packages, chips of ceramic, lottery tickets that won nothing. Penniless, I start out again like everyone else.

## Mark Halperin

Buying a Dictionary

It may have been a little expensive by Russian standards, but when I found the four-volume Dictionary of the Russian Language, the "academia nauk" edition, long out of print, I was thrilled. I handed over all the money I had on me, and gladly. That eagerness surprised the sales-girl, who had taken it out of the locked display case to show me and who had stood beside me, watching as I fingered the pages. But by the time I returned from the cashier, receipt in hand, she too seemed to take pleasure in my happiness. She carefully wrapped the volumes in stout brown "butcher" paper, tied the package with twine, twice, and walked with me to the store exit, not far from the old KGB building and its notorious underground prison and torture center. I wasn't thinking of the weight, those four green volumes with their gold lettered spines and covers. I was reveling in possessing them, and marched to the metro, fished out a jeton, for the turnstile, pushed through and walked to the platform. Though it wasn't yet rush hour, all seats in the car were taken. I must have been smiling—dead give-away of the foreigner—but the seated woman I was standing in front of looked up and asked "heavy package?" And still flushed with the thrill of the books, I replied, "the four volume Academy dictionary." If that meant nothing to her, my joy was so contagious it didn't matter. She offered to hold them on her lap. At my stop, when she handed them back, I said, "thank you," and, cradling the books, smiled all the way to my room.

**Pablo Neruda**

## Ceremony

In 1847 an American vessel, the clipper "Cymbelina," landed in some nameless cove in northern Chile. There the men of the sea proceeded to take down the figurehead from the prow of the sailing vessel. This white and gold statue seemed to be a very young bride garbed in Elizabethan costume. The face of that wooden girl was astonishing because of its wrenching beauty. The seamen of the "Cymbelina" had mutinied. They maintained that the prow figurehead moved its eyes during the voyage, putting them off course and terrifying the crew.

It is not an easy thing to dethrone the queen of a tough, old vessel. But, impelled by that religious terror, the sailors sawed through the powerful bolt that fastened it to the bowsprit, cut through nails and screws until they were able, not without certain fear or respect, to lower it and place it in a launch that carried it to shore.

The sea was choppy that July day. It was the middle of winter, and a heavy, slow rain, strange in that desert-like region, was falling on the world.

Seven crewmen carried on their shoulders the wooden girl strangely separated from her ship. Then they dug a ditch in the sand. The guanayes, stercoraceous coastal birds, were flying in circles, cawing and shrieking while the unsettling chore lasted. They laid her on the ground and covered her with the nitrous sand of the desert. It isn't known if any of the men who buried her attempted to pray or felt some sudden pang of regret or sadness. The garuga, a slow rain borne on the north wind that oscillates between fog and phantasmagoria, soon covered the seashore, the yellow cliffs, and the boat which in the great silence brought the seafarers back to the sailing ship "Cymbelina" on that morning in July 1847.

*translated by Dennis Maloney and Clark M. Zlotchew*

## Peter Johnson

### Hawk

Sometimes I awake with a headline stuck in my head: Doctor in Bangor Treating Elvis for Migraines; Pharmacist Completes History of Drive-In Movie Theater—and I write it all down in my little red notebook. But there are other nights when blood rocks my heart, and people I've injured or the dead appear, hovering above the ceiling fan. The city is asleep, the city is awake, the city is napping. Does it matter? I think, climbing insomnia's creaky stairs to an attic that doesn't exist, trying to remember what is good, what is right. Yesterday, my student fell from a tree and died. That morning I knelt before the dog's crate and kissed her goodbye. I stopped to buy cough drops and a backscratcher. I was cut off twice and beeped at once. My student wrote a story about the Civil War, about heroism. He wrote about an uprising of Christmas reindeer, about a boy and his imaginary camel. He drew a cartoon called the "Devolution of Man," and he once wrote: "Artists have to try, no matter how hard to love their enemy because it is up to artists to save humanity." Because he believed in what he wrote, he wasn't my best writer. He wasn't a liar, he wasn't waiting for applause. The clap of crows emptying a tree was enough for him, the simple architecture of an egg. He had climbed, I think, to gain a different perspective, like the hawk that mysteriously appeared today. I was walking to class and sensed his dracular presence, then heard a squirrel's lament no more than ten feet away—a bone-crushing sorrow for life, for death.

## Ana Delgadillo

### Surrounding My Birth in Veracruz

I'm sure I heard the plane's roar through my mother's abdomen, hitting my small upside-down ears. My parents waved their goodbyes through the coconut palms of Veracruz. My uncle was flying north with the geese. Sometimes I can still feel my head throb where it bumped into the crest of my mother's pelvis as she got into the car to leave the airport. She was anxious to get home, to get away from the fumes. I ricocheted clumsily within her like a pebble during the earthquake in Oaxaca that marked the day of my birth. The car crossed the city line and headed over the bridge where the Jamapa River's mouth tastes the saltiness of the sea, reaching the road canopied by mango trees, from Tinajas to Tierra Blanca. Oaxaca's only an hour away but still too far from home. My mother scrunched up in the back seat felt our connection, a pearl within an oyster in a smoked metal can. A red truck passed by as another truck overtook us. Shots broke loose like cannons from the truck, fired at the men fleeing. My legs touched the tip of my nose as my father thrust my mother's head between her knees, all because the poor were just trying to get away from being poor.

My mother says she could feel me searching for an opening so I could see. I wanted to see. I wanted to know. I pushed my head through, opening her womb like a window. My mother still remembers the pain. My father rushed us to the nearest hospital, where seventeen years later I would watch my grandfather die. The hospital floor remembers me. It remembers my father's worried steps, his snakeskin boots bruising the linoleum tiles. It remembers the earth shaking.

## Sean Mclain Brown

tag·mem·ics: (tæg ′ mēm iks)

In the last days on the farm, my brothers struggled with the pigs, their arms bulging like ropes, shoulders arcing and straining under the weight. The hard part is killing them, but we needed the money. They stood ankle-deep in mud and shit, and flipped coins for the rifle and chainsaw. Standing on my tiptoes, I watched from the window of my room.

My brothers stood over the pigs like twin gods, their muscled backs toward me, things tucked into a back moment enough, flesh-colored and smelling like rotting wood and mold. Brittle bones like razor coral, some hearts and organs, and later that day in town, the church's steeple rising like a spear, and the thank yous to the Lord for his bounty, sanctioned by measured nods, something about a mighty sea parting, significance and miracles.

And the things we lost; a one-arm hired hand with two children walking away from our house, headlights driving down the road, sloping light across our fields, one-hundred acres, twenty-three chickens, a few horses, a father, a farm, my life.

**Daryl Scroggins**

## Holiday

On Easter Sundays I find a sunny chair and read the poems of Wallace Stevens. What a thing to celebrate—Easter: cyclical time ended by the first unique event. And yet, as Easter rolls around again, a new batch of little dresses heads for the church across the street. Boys tug at collars and are slapped with white gloves. I see them all from my window, and hear the bells, same as always. I drink mimosas. And then comes the best part. The kids saunter out, and for a moment an old decorum, enforced by their mothers, prevents them from running. The women gently commiserate; the men adroitly fetch the cars. And then the children, finally released, take up stones against their own kind.

## Cecilia Woloch

### My Mother's Birds

My mother's Polish nickname was Sucha, the word for dry. Dried-up, her mother called her; little witch; Miss Skin-and-Bones. Fifth of eleven thin and startled children; all those mouths to feed. They baked potatoes over fires in the street, so I've been told; dipped stale bread in buttermilk; ate what was put in front of them. So what? — it was the Great Depression; everyone was poor. And my mother—dark-eyed, dreamy—tied her black hair up in rags. Played movie-star in vacant lots. High-kicked through cinders, broken glass. Collected cigarette butts for the pennies Dzia-dzia gave. Though CioaCia Helen down the hill, their crazy aunt, was better off. She gave them sweets, cheap sweets but sweet. She gave them Easter chicks one year. My mother took the tiny peeps and raised them tenderly, as pets. I've seen the photographs: their white wings seem to rise out of her arms. As if such chickens could have flown, but they were meat, those birds she loved. Tough meat, and these were hungry years. And CioaCia raised the axe. My mother sobbed and couldn't swallow, nor could anyone, I've heard. The story goes she saved a few stray feathers, hid them, sang to them. Knelt above them weeping in the attic, just like church. Fed and watered them for months, her sisters laughed; the ghosts of birds. And so, years later, always singing, she would try to fatten us. Her own strange brood of seven children, raised less tenderly, perhaps. As if, this time, she wanted to be sure we'd get away. She'd set the steaming plates in front of us, still humming, cross her arms. Don't be afraid to eat, she'd say. Because we were, we were afraid.

## Kenneth Koch

### On Happiness

It was distressing to think that Kawabata had committed suicide. It wasn't distressing, however, to find out that he had defined happiness as drinking a scotch and soda at the Tokyo Hilton Hotel. An acquaintance of mine thought this was terrible thing to say, to such an extent that for him it seemed almost to destroy the value of Kawabata's work.

Sitting on the terrace of the Hilton!

What's wrong with that?

A friend of mine, a woman, once explained happiness to me.

We were sitting in the Place de la Republique in Paris, an unlikely spot for happiness. We were tired, had walked a lot, had sat down at a large, generic big-square café. Dear though it may be to its proprietors and its habitués, it seemed ordinary enough to us. So we sat there and she ordered a Beaujolais and I, a beer. After two swallows of the beer, I was overcome by a feeling of happiness. I told her and I told again about it later.

She had a theory about a "happiness base." Once, she said, you had this base, at odd times, moments of true happiness could occur.

Without this base, however, they would not.

The base was made of good health, good work, good friendship, good love. Of course, you can have all these and not be "happy."

You have to have the base, and then be lucky, she said. That's why you were happy at the café.

Kawabata asked my acquaintance in turn: How would you define happiness? He told me his answer: "I said 'How can anyone answer a question like that?'"

## James Wright

### Honey

My father died at the age of eighty. One of the last things he did in his life was to call his fifty-eight-year-old son-in-law "honey." One afternoon in the early 1930's, when I bloodied my head by pitching over a wall at the bottom of a hill and believed that the mere sight of my own blood was the tragic meaning of life, I heard my father offer to murder his future son-in-law. His son-in-law is my brother-in-law, whose name is Paul. These two grown men rose above and knew that human life is murder. They weren't fighting with each other because one strong man, a factory worker, was laid off from his work, and the other strong man, the driver of a coral truck, was laid off from his work. They were both determined to live their lives, and so they glared at each other and said they were going to live, come hell or high water. High water is not trite in southern Ohio. Nothing is trite along a river. My father died a good death. To die a good death means to live one's life. I don't say a good life.

I say a life.

## Carolyn Forché

### The Colonel

What you have heard is true. I was in his house. His wife carried a tray of coffee and sugar. His daughter filed her nails, his son went out for the night. There were daily papers, pet dogs, a pistol on the cushion beside him. The moon swung bare on its black cord over the house. On the television was a cop show. It was in English. Broken bottles were embedded in the walls around the house to scoop the kneecaps from a man's legs or cut his hands to lace. On the windows there were gratings like those in liquor stores. We had dinner, rack of lamb, good wine, a gold bell was on the table for calling the maid. The maid brought green mangoes, salt, a type of bread. I was asked how I enjoyed the country. There was a brief commercial in Spanish. His wife took everything away. There was some talk of how difficult it had become to govern. The parrot said hello on the terrace. The colonel told it to shut up, and pushed himself from the table. My friend said to me with his eyes: say nothing. The colonel returned with a sack used to bring groceries home. He spilled many human ears on the table. They were like dried peach halves. There is not other way to say this. He took one of them in his hands, shook it in our faces, dropped it into a water glass. It came alive there. I am tired of fooling around he said. As for the rights of anyone, tell your people they can go fuck themselves. He swept the ears to the floor with his arm and held the last of his wine in the air. Something for your poetry, no? he said. Some of the ears on the floor caught this scrap of his voice. Some of the ears on the floor were pressed to the ground.

## Object Poems

This strategy is much used by prose poets and (free) verse poets alike, most famously by Rainer Maria Rilke in his "Dinggedichten" (thing poems) and by Francis Ponge. In most object poems, the poet attempts to "get out of the way" of the description and of the language in order to discover an essential observation about the object itself or about the language one must use to talk about the object. Ponge, for example, seeks to observe objects so intensely and exhaustively that the description "rises to the level of meditation." The language of the object poem, therefore, tends to be objective and concrete, but there are exceptions: Morton Marcus chooses to describe an object of little physical presence in "Mathematics" and resorts to imaginative flights based on the shapes of numbers; Brenda Hillman uses a combination of geometric and botanical jargon, editorialization, and painterly metaphor to depict the White Fir in a clinical manner that sets up, by contrast, the touching final line; Peter Redgrove's evocation of granite rises as much from his discussion of granite's genesis as of its appearance; stones in the hands of Gabriella Mistral give up their most human aspects; Jesse Lee Kercheval's description of an unfamiliar fruit turns into much more—a meditation on memory and strangeness—via associations with the taste, color, and texture of the fruit; and Miroslav Holub and Nin Andrews use as much imagination as observation in their consideration of teeth and the orgasm, respectively.

## Francis Ponge

### The Orange

Like the sponge, the orange aspires to regain face after enduring the ordeal of expression. But where the sponge always succeeds, the orange never does; for its cells have burst, its tissues are torn. While the rind alone is flabbily recovering its form, thanks to its resilience, an amber liquid has oozed out, accompanied, as we know, by sweet refreshment, sweet perfume but also by the bitter awareness of a premature expulsion of pips as well.

Must one take sides between these two poor ways of enduring oppression? The sponge is only a muscle and fills up with air, clean or dirty water, whatever: a vile exercise. The orange has better taste, but is too passive—and this fragrant sacrifice is really too great a kindness to the oppressor.

However, merely recalling its singular manner of perfuming the air and delighting its tormentor is not saying enough about the orange. One has to stress the glorious color of the resulting liquid which, more than lemon juice, makes the larynx open widely both to pronounce the word and ingest the juice without any apprehensive grimace of the mouth or raising of papillae.

And one remains speechless to declare the well-deserved admiration of the covering of the tender, fragile, russet oval ball inside that thick moist blotter, whose extremely thin but highly pigmented skin, bitterly flavorful, is just uneven enough to catch the light worthily on its perfect fruit form.

At the end of too brief a study, conducted as roundly as possible, one has to get down to the pip. This seed, shaped like a miniature lemon, is the color of the lemon tree's whitewood outside, and inside is the green of a pea or tender sprout. It is within this seed that one finds—after the sensational explosion of the Chinese lantern of flavors, colors and perfumes which is the fruited ball itself—the relative hardness and greenness (not entirely tasteless, by the way) of the wood, the branch, the leaf; in short, the puny albeit prime purpose of the fruit.

*translated by Beth Archer Brombert*

## Peter Redgrove

### Granite Gazing

Granite cannot burn: it transforms. As the lava pushes through the stone gates, the granite of them, encountering the vehement temperatures, projects a metamorphic aureole, like a rainbowing bruise of its body. Our county is made of this aureole of rocks. The primal granite is like the bones of God which quake to the movement of stars. You can see the stars glittering in the stone; it is an observatory. But the creatory of the mother accords more easily, and it was for this reason that the deities entered the human womb, that is, for easier breathing, of a more competent amplitude, and not plunged into the womb of rock that gives only one hundredth of a millimetre to the passage of the moon. Now the harmonious beating of the hearts of mother and child accord. She raises her sail, like big-bellied Isis. She raises her soul, and the granite cliffs begin to flow. She carries the child lightly, and thus, with a simple movement, such as this raising of her sail, can move the world in its entirety.

## Gabriella Mistral

### In Praise of Stones

Kneeling stones, stones falling in cavalcades, and those never wanting to fall, like a heart become too weary.

Stones resting on their shoulders like dead warriors—their wounds are sealed with pure silence, not with bandages.

Stones hold scattered gestures like lost children: an eyebrow on the sierra, an ankle in a stone bench.

Stones remember a unified face and want to piece it back together, gesture by gesture, someday.

Stones heavy with sleep, rich with dreams, like a peppercorn guarding pure essence, languid and drowsy, like a tree of conjunctures, stone savagely clutches it treasure of absolute dreams.

Kneeling stones, commingled stones, stones falling in cavalcades, and those not wanting to fall, like a heart become too weary.

The headstone destined for Jacob's neck, the stone of mourning is like a number—without a blush and without dew—it is just like a number.

Round stone is simply a great eyelid, with eyelashes, like Methuselah's. The hooked summit of the mystical Andes, that flame that doesn't dance, halted abruptly like Lot's wife Sarah. It did not want to answer me when I was a child, and it still does not answer me.

Stones flashing with gold or silver, suddenly pierced by copper, are startled by the intrusion. Stones are irritated by metallic almonds, as though they were invisible darts.

Kneeling stones, commingled stones, stones running in phalanxes or throngs, without arriving anywhere.

Ancient river stones from slippery shores are like the drowned—they hold the same withered vegetation that sticks fast to the hair of the drowned. But tender stones exist; they can touch someone who has been flayed and not hurt him. They pass over his body with a tongue like this own mother's, and they don't grow tired.

Young river stones are pebbles painted like fruit. Yes, they can sing! Once, when I was also five years old, I placed them under my pillow; they made a commotion like a mountain of tots being smothered, or perhaps they took turns singing a round at the nucleus of my dream. They were its masters: tender-aged pebbles came to my sheets and played with me.

Some stones do not want to become tombstones or fountains; they shun a foreign touch and refuse the intrusive inscription in order to make their own gestures, unique language, rise someday.

Mute stones, their hearts are bestowed with a passion that could be given away. In order not to disturb the slumber of their vertiginous almond—only for that reason, they remain still.

*translated by Maria Giachetti*

## Jesse Lee Kercheval

### Italy, October

To be here is to be where fruit you have never seen before grows on equally strange trees. The fruit is not, as you first thought, oranges, though it is orange in color. Nor is it a tangerine or some strangely colored apple. Then you see it in the market, each soft fruit cradled in its own nest of woven plastic. Kaki, the sign reads, 200 lire. You hold out a palm of silver, and let the cashier pick warm coins from your waiting hand. Then she wraps your kaki in white paper like a present, which you carry to your hotel, hoping kaki can be safely eaten raw.

In your room, you slice it open, lift the kaki to your lips and find it sweeter than any fruit you've ever tasted, half watermelon, half pressed roses. Only when you've finished do you think to look up kaki in your pocket Italian dictionary, which says it means persimmon. And you remember as a child picking a persimmon at a friend's house, then leaving it all afternoon in your mother's stand-up freezer. Still, when you bit the unripe fruit, your mouth drew up in a pucker from which you—silent person that you are—never did recover. Until today in Sacile when you took a bite of strange fruit.

Now, who knows? You may speak in tongues.

**Brenda Hillman**

## White Fir Description

—14 cones at the top with meso-tight rings of fitted pods, boy bronzes rising somewhat

—The usual turkey-foot top but with toes splayed 43°, 47°, 49°

—At no place does the sun show through more politeness than 8-inch rhombuses criss-crossed with daggerdowns, & the "wrestle" "with my heart" side

—Each needle an inch-and-a-half more profuse toward manzanita than near Meeks Bay more profane toward sound of scrub jay stopping then doubling

—Changeoid quiver-cripple wind starts up & lets you record: how often you fought a fear, half-panic laced with ennui as

—Blond oxygen hovers over the tree, in the direness of safety—an ethics that would want to want the other to get better

## Morton Marcus

### Mathematics

The number 1 wanders alone in his short-brimmed cap at the edge of the sunlit field. I love him because he is pure, because he is all ego and all beginning, because he concentrates on himself and all first causes, in perpetual solitude: the one sun, the one field; the one tree, and squirrel; the one bobcat. One is the archetype of archetypes, the soul of souls struggling to comprehend the soul of the tree, the essence of the bobcat. No wonder he is the namer of plants and animals.

And I am overjoyed with the number 2; its long swan neck entrances me. It is exotic in the same way anything encountered for the first time is exotic. But it provides an even greater pleasure because it is the other side of 1, the part he could not see but always knew was there—the part suggested by his shadow. 2 is the night sky to one's daylit field. 2 is the coupling of two ones, the merging of two solitudes, the second of two eyes which allows the head to see two realities, the realities of the right and the left sides.

But I am more excited by the infant shape of 3 than by the shapes of 1 and 2 put together. Can that be? Yes, because 3 is the child of the first two, the combination of both, the offspring beyond their egos. It plays in the field of its father, it reaches for the stars of its mother.

All progressions proceed from the number 3.

## Nin Andrews

### Notes on the Orgasm

The orgasm is your invisible counterpart. She goes out in the world, wreaking havoc.

The orgasm knows all things are animate. The houses groan with grief and passion. Sometimes a mirror bursts from a wall and shatters, no longer content with mere images.

The orgasm tells you to be careful or, in the language of orgasms, to have fears. Orgasms thrive on danger.

The orgasm says we are all parts of herself. We are but launching pads for her spiritual development. After she is done with us, she will be ready for fucking angels.

The orgasm encourages us to let our minds wander. Usually this is good advice, but sometimes she gets lost in thought.

When the orgasm tells you that you are a mere object of her scientific research and the only real man on earth, the orgasm is slowly dissecting your body.

The orgasm will peel you like an orange. You may feel exposed, raw, even wounded. The orgasm wants you to live life without the rind.

The orgasm thinks people are like dresses. You don't just buy the first one off the rack. You try them on for size.

The orgasm tells you many stories. Some she will never finish. She cannot help herself. She always lies. Such beautiful lies. You want them all. Why would you need truth when you can have an orgasm?

Every now and then a casualty occurs. An orgasm accidentally injures or murders a man. She is startled by the moans escaping from his lips at this moment, so much like those of pleasure. She wonders if human pain is a kind of celebration.

Sometimes the orgasm falls in love with you. She cannot tear herself from your pungent flesh. For days you walk around, gasping for air. You are in a state of constant excitement. One day the orgasm abandons you. The entire world is reduced to a memory, a mere elegy to an orgasm.

In a single sitting a hungry orgasm can consume a man, socks and all. Women take more time.

Many dislike the speed of orgasm, the way she comes and goes and takes all she can get. The orgasm cannot help herself. She has no tomorrow.

According to the orgasm, there is no difference between real and imaginary events. Everything is a secret message only she can decipher.

Often the orgasm tells you a story about you. About you and about the secret powers lying dormant within you. She waits for you on street corners and follows you down dark alleys, whispering your name, softly, her hands passing continually over your hair, caressing your bare shoulders. At night you sleep fitfully and dream of her. You are unable to tell whether you are dream of the orgasm, or if the orgasm is a dream of you.

The orgasm is very happy to be an orgasm. Sometimes she wonders what it would be like to be a man, sort of like the small boy who fills a Mason jar with spiders, wondering what it's like to be a fly.

## Miroslav Holub

### Teeth

Teeth are a rather ridiculous inside remnant of the outside. Their life is filled with dread that they'll be forced outside again and lost there. A lost tooth doesn't know if it's clenched or revealed in a smile, it doesn't know how to put down roots and so it loses its capacity for aching.

Many teeth have been lost throughout the history of civilization, some by educational and corrective measures in the lives of younger individuals, some by the wasting away of old age. Teeth that have been bashed in during the development of civilizations don't rot, they scurry along in the darkness, scared of daylight. Some just grow tired, and are discovered and described in some new scientific discipline.

Surviving teeth convene on dark cloudy evenings, trembling with horror and telling the old gum stories, fist stories, stories of stiff boots, of other kinds of bashing. These stories are not without some unintentional comic effects, the teeth become comic figures, repeating their plots evening after evening, century after century.

That's how the puppet theater came about.

It's the theater of teeth, for which there's no mouth.

Now close your mouths, children, and listen.

*translated by Dana Hábova and Stuart Friebert*

## Central Image/Central Object

In this strategy the poem is built around a dominant image or object. Generally, the object is developed through evolving detail, and the reader's understanding or appreciation of the image is gradually enhanced as the poem progresses. In some poems the central image or object is used figuratively, implying metaphorical nuances that might not be immediately understood at the poem's onset. Other poems use the image as a unifying factor for actions or emotions anchored to the object.

Leonard Schwartz uses the imagery of the natural world—leaves, oranges, the moon—as the central objects of his poem "The Stream." Each new line of the poem seems almost to spring from the seed planted in the line before it. The observations in the poem gradually accumulate to something like an epiphany of place in the world. Poet Maxine Chernoff takes a decidedly different approach in her poem "Origin," using the dreamlike imagery of an ancestral home to arrive, not unlike Schwartz though by different paths, at an image that suggests the speaker has a role in the machine of the universe. James Schuyler's "Footnote" is a lovely meditation on the bluet. This poem might serve as a good distinction from the Object Poem, in that the focus of the Object Poem is observation of an object, whereas Schuyler here is as much concerned with the word "bluet" and its sound as he is with any object to which the word refers (though we could easily have considered this poem an Object Poem by simply stipulating that a word is an object). George Kalamaras's "Williams in the Hospital, 1952," like many ekphrastic poems (poems about other works of art), uses a photograph as an imaginative leaping-off point.

**Leonard Schwartz**

## The Stream

The stream needs me to be here to run through this meadow and there is no humiliation in being a patch of ground, nor is there dread in the heart of the angel upon realizing his wings are spread in a tar pit.

All these leaves setting up shop on my easel are entirely a matter of my own expectation. Yes, but if you canoe by the right open window, a government will be seen giving itself to someone else, which would explain why this year summer is leaving us out.

Think of it as too much heat, so much sunburn saved. I would have been naked, right? Haven't I always been kind of frowning with flame, like all those woods evidently still wintering, still hesitant about getting into the foliage?

OK, I concede that love never outgrows the forest of the maternal, those thickets in which the dunce of language loses himself.

OK, oranges are gleaming sources.

Nothing will ever wrangle those oranges from the trees, groves and groves of them.

An almost muscular moon suddenly experiences an earthquake, ivory keyboards first picking up a vibration that squishes and rages and rats on us.

A ray of sunlight picks the moon right from the sky.

I'm just one raspberry falling into the cup.

## Maxine Chernoff

### Origin

Cloudy as a picture of a relative so distant I must squint to see him on the pea-colored photo: Manchuria, 1908. And oh, the train ride. The steppes so beautiful in spring with reindeer dancing *pas de deux*. The European bittern making fence repairs with its hammer head. Caviar in cut glass bowls. The Yellow Sea so blue it must have been named by jaundiced men. Iron mines springing up everywhere like hot dog stands. I'll make the Ural Mountains my coat-of-arms. Under white exploding stars, I'll find my ancient cousins playing dominoes. I'll sleep on raspberry seats, the shiny steel tracks receding under me like childhood.

A dream of a train so small my window is a postage stamp. Through the Manchurian countryside, I watch the stars fade out one by one, metal ducks in a carnival shooting arcade.

**James Schuyler**

## Footnote

The bluet is a small flower, creamy-throated, that grows in patches in New England lawns. The bluet (French pronunciation) is the shaggy cornflower, growing wild in France. "The Bluet" is a poem I wrote. The Bluet is a painting of Joan Mitchell's. The thick blue runs and holds. All of them, broken-up pieces of sky, hard sky, soft sky. Today I'll take Joan's giant vision, running and holding, staring you down with beauty. Though I need reject none. Bluet. "Bloo-ay."

## George Kalamaras

### Williams in the Hospital, 1952

*based on a photograph by Alfred Eisenstaedt*

I found it in a rare book, water-marked and stained, that photograph of William Carlos Williams and an infant looking back at the good doctor, blurry-eyed and weeping. Williams' left hand consolingly on its right elbow, his mouth open as if to say *Googly-goo. Now what's wrong with you?* This profile of Williams' dark furry brow arched above glasses that study the multiple causes of pain. The beginning of the world and its untimely end. The infant stares back, mouth held in horror at the good doctor's touch, a perpetual wail wrangling from its prune-faced scowl. Its tiny ribs exposed like the breathing flank of a young zebra, stunned and panting fifty years through the black and white film. The sternum expanded and strained from the strength of so much weeping. Is it a little boy- or little girl-scream I see, forcing its frown forever into Williams' brow? Bare-chested wrangler who might one day grow up to herd cattle, dance ballet, hoist iron from a 13th floor scaffold. Who might one day bend to tenderly kiss a child of its own, try to calm it from some other terrible blight. Williams keeps leaning toward it, toward me, with fatherly concern, his white coat bunched at the collar, the knot in his necktie a way to make visible that knot hidden in his throat. His stethoscope sways like an unattached organ. He keeps holding the arm of the tiny child like the handle of a moving mirror. He steadies himself in the study, hears his first name perpetually echoed in his last. *It's okay, googly-goo*, he says. *Who are You?*

## Extended/Controlling Metaphor

The extended metaphor is quite simply a metaphor drawn out over much or all of a poem. It allows the poet to sustain an initial comparison or equation until it resonates beyond the restraints of the original association. The controlling metaphor builds upon the association by allowing the metaphor to shape the poem as an organizing principle, or a kind of backbone. The reader may be engaged by a single metaphor which, as it is developed, soon gives way to multiple, overlapping points of similarity gradually blossoming through the poem.

"When It All Comes Down to the Last Resort" by Paul Dickey employs one of the great American metaphors: sports. Dickey chooses baseball, America's national pastime, as the context for a deceptively complex metaphor extended perhaps even to the point of allegory. Chad Davidson brings together relationships and woodworking in his poem "Refinishing," turning the poem in the end on the image of the splinter. Kyle Vaughn begins his poem by comparing time to a piece of paper; then, like an origami artist, he continues to bend and shape the metaphor, and the poem itself, until he arrives at a conclusion that is both unexpected and surprisingly beautiful. Joe Ahearn's "My Superpowers" uses the *X-Men* lingo of mutants and powers, implicitly comparing the superman to the ordinary man in a meditation on what it means to be human. Jamey Dunham's "Poem With Weasels, ca. 1930 (Black and White)" puts weasels in the place of humans as a way of approaching the absurdity of identity conflicts such as racial profiling. Robert Bly's poem "Warning to the Reader" compares the plight of birds caught in a granary to readers seeking false hope within the darkness of a poem. Like many poems in this anthology, the Bly poem might easily fit into another category—in this case, the poem of address.

## Paul Dickey

*When it All Comes Down to the Last Resort*

Our star reliever is truth although on occasion we may keep him warming up in the bullpen, rest his knuckleball, doubt that he exists, fine him for showing up late for pre-games, consult with the general manager about our options on his contract. After all, dear, it is our life and no, we didn't mean to have it all happen like this.

So what right does he have signing autographs for the kids to sleep with when we may be going into extra innings? I admit, he sleeps with the third baseman's wife. The manager knows these things, but I have a team to think of.

## Kyle Vaughn

### Letter to My Imagined Daughter

If I could fold this lonely year in half and then in half again, until finally it became next year, I would keep folding until I came to where you are. I would keep folding until this year made a little paper car. This white car would be soft, like a cloud in the air. And even more than a soft cloud, this would be a bright car, more like the sun in the middle of the day. And as it does through certain glass, its light would keep folding, folding in—making the world spin like a red barber's chair, once around for every fast ray.

## Chad Davidson

### Refinishing

Wood has no future. It saves all scratches. At twenty-three I helped a woman sand her table down to grain. I touched every inch of that table, used a belt-sander but took the corners by hand, not wanting to burn through. I had it clean in days, then set to clearcoating. I could count my years in its surface as the tiny histories of the people who had eaten there vanished.

When we lie together at night and I'm asleep, do I ever run my fingers down your back? I have the sensation sometimes of running underneath the skin, like a splinter.

## Joe Ahearn

### My Superpowers

Could the sacred, whatever its variants, be a two-sided formation? One aspect founded in murder and the other in common human genetics?

In my case, the mutations resulted in superpowers. I could no longer control my body's attraction to metal. Even now merely the thought of magnetic fields causes me endless pain.

Understanding one's superpowers is the discovery of a circle which, via both poles, endlessly rejoins itself. Life and death become fused in an isolated plastic cell, suspended invisibly above the graying traffic.

We mutants have always found ourselves socially ostracized and alienated by these new characteristics. We have no hold on the others but one woven of fright and repulsion.

One hears the stories. He is the combinatorial fly-human. He is the limit of bare existence. His need for fresh air and open space is stronger than any hatred. If his mind can travel the globe, what difference does it make if his legs work? His mouth chews a hole in the word.

But let me tell you, no matter how different, we mutants still gather omens in the street, just like you.

*Homo sapiens* into *homo sapiens* into *homo sapiens* into *homo sapiens sapiens.* Something as immaterial as language, yet earthly, terrestrial, a new living dead man, a new power, *sapiens logodracula*. Something as immaterial as language, yet earthly, terrestrial, a new power, which may not involve them, manifests itself. Something as immaterial as language, yet earthly, terrestrial, a new sacred man.

**Jamey Dunham**

## Poem with Weasels, ca. 1930s (Black and White)

Two weasels settle into their seats at the back of the movie house and wait for the serial to begin. As the screen crackles to life, they are presented with the image of a weasel as portrayed by a mink. The actor is dressed in a long striped sweater that hugs its slender frame like a sweatsock. It wears a large wool cap pulled down over its beady eyes. As the weasel slinks across the stage, popping in and out of darkened alleys, it is accompanied by an organ playing the ominous theme of the "bad guy." Finally, the creature stops and cranes its long, plastic neck around a corner. Outside the candy store, a child sits alone on a park bench, clutching an oversized lollipop. The weasel licks its whiskers, rubs its hands together like a fly. A clamor of hisses and boos erupt from the audience and the two weasels decide to slip out the exit.

Outside the temperature has dropped noticeably. One of the weasels turns up the collar of its coat and is immediately aware of looking conspicuous. Across the street, a black child sits on a shoeshine box, swinging his legs and smearing shoe polish on his face. He pauses to look at his reflection in a store window, then smiles and dabs on a bit more. An enormous poodle bursts from the gates of the city park, its middle-aged owner in tow. The two are a fantastic spectacle of curls, pearls and mink. The woman frantically flails her shopping bags, trying desperately to keep her footing on four-inch heels, but each new square of concrete finds her closer and closer to disaster. Finally, she is lifted from the pavement like a kite and sent sprawling into the street. A cop appears to help her to her feet, then turns to face the weasels. Slowly the officer approaches, thumping his nightstick like a farmer knocking dirt from a turnip. The weasels stop. The first instinctively drops its eyes to its feet, begins nervously smoothing down its collar. The second hesitates, then cautiously steps forward. With a nod to the officer, it motions over at the young child whose white smile slowly dissolves into his shiny black face.

## Robert Bly

### Warning to the Reader

Sometimes farm granaries become especially beautiful when all the oats or wheat are gone, and wind has swept the rough floor clean. Standing inside, we see around us, coming through the cracks between shrunken wall boards, bands or strips of sunlight. So in a poem about imprisonment, one sees a little light.

But how many birds have died trapped in these granaries. The bird, seeing freedom in the light, flutters up the wall and falls back again and again. The way out is where the rats enter and leave; but the rat's hole is low to the floor. Writer, be careful then by showing the sunlight on the walls not to promise the anxious and panicky blackbirds a way out!

I say to the reader, beware. Readers who love poems of light may sit hunched in the corner with nothing in their gizzards for four days, light failing, the eyes glazed...

They may end as a mound of feathers and a skull on the open boardwood floor...

## Meditation

The meditative prose poem is similar to the poems of Extended/Controlling Metaphor and Central Image/Central Object in that it tends to revolve around a central idea, memory, or subject that is turned over and over in the mind of the speaker. It may use elements of the Anecdote or other strategies such as Variation on a Theme in service of its goal to arrive somewhere new in its contemplation of the subject at hand. It also tends to be a more intimate strategy, since the meditative poem frequently purports to be the private thoughts of the poet him or her self. At the less intimate extreme of the spectrum, where the privately spoken poem crosses over into public utterance, the meditative poem may cross over into Rant territory.

Brian Johnson's "Self-Portrait (Kneeling)," one of his several poems in a "Self-Portrait" sequence, takes the nature of the self as its central subject and talks around it, considering many things that seem not to be the self as a way of finding that the self is all of these things. David Lazar's "Goodness Knows" ruminates over several memories as a poignant way of wondering how the speaker got to the point where he finds himself in the present. Phyllis Koestenbaum's "Young Armless Man in a Barbeque Restaurant" takes a flight of imagination sparked by a chance encounter as the point of its meditation, eventually revealing to us that the meditation has gone on for "more than two years," so that the poem—like many poems—is a kind of distillation of much longer, deeper, prior meditation.

## Brian Johnson

### Self-Portrait (Kneeling)

I pray that I continue to love the resemblance of things. When the rocks become human nipples, wheat becomes the spines of fish, the trees are a family of wooden kings, and the train from Istanbul arrives at noon, dressed as a bride, I have no questions.

I pray to the cinematic flame. It is a turn, a moment of uneasiness, the first time alone in a foreign country. The faces are strange and unto themselves, like the birds nested in their towers. I walk on the painted glass and watch the monks reading.

Before sleep, I stare at my name in the light. I search the mosaic for inscriptions. A group of musicians is visible in the center, with a goddess twisting her nearly translucent hair over someone lying on a bed. There is a carafe, and hills.

I am like mumbling in the woodshed, the prayer without name, or origin, I am similar to that. Like a horse neighing out its state of loneliness, the hunter looking for his wife's hand, the snowfall, the indifferent river, I am that.

Roman tombstone, pagan script, table, soul, and screen: nothing is left to children. You emerge from the wood talking of miracles, thermal springs and fish-stocked ponds. And here is the oldest game: the sun putting on the robe, putting the robe and leaving.

## Phyllis Koestenbaum

### Young Armless Man in the Barbecue Restaurant

The hostess seats a girl and a young man in a short-sleeve sport shirt with one arm missing below the shoulder. I'm at the next table with my husband and son, Andy's Barbecue Restaurant, an early evening in July, chewing a boneless rib eye, gulping a dark beer ordered from the cocktail waitress, a nervous woman almost over the hill, whose high heel sandals click back and forth from the bar to the dining room joined to the bar by an open arch. A tall heavy cook in white hat is brushing sauce on the chicken and spareribs rotating slowly on a squeaking spit. Baked potatoes heat on the oven floor. The young man is eating salad with his one hand. He and his girl are on a date. He has a forties' movie face, early Van Johnson before the motorcycle accident scarred his forehead. He lost the arm recently. Hard as it is, it could be worse. I would even exchange places with him if I could. *I want to exchange places with the young armless man in the barbecue restaurant.* He would sit at my table and I would sit at his. After dinner I would go in his car and he would go in mine. I would live in his house and work at his job and he would live in my house and do what I do. I would be him dressing and undressing and he would be me dressing and undressing. Our bill comes. My husband leaves the tip on the tray; we take toothpicks and mints and walk through the dark workingman's bar out to the parking lot still lit by the sky though the streetlights have come on as they do automatically at the same time each night. We drive our son, home for the summer, back to his job at the bookstore. As old Italians and Jews say of sons from five to fifty, he's a good boy. I have worked on this paragraph for more than two years.

**David Lazar**

## Goodness Knows

Radical is Latin for root, and each morning I pull myself out of bed and root for my better side to stay buried. When I was a boy, Mrs. Hall, from down the hall, would pull her Johnny up the stairs and say why couldn't he be like me, "always the straight and narrow." Mother closed the door behind me so father's strange song stayed inside.

When I was with the Brothers, I longed to be a single taper, the first vesper in the dark mornings. Brother Anthony's voice would caress mine during the Sanctus, sliding vowels under my deepest piety.

Now I run some rum, and sometimes a sip or two will give me a vision of a worldly world with the trappings of a paradise, which I've always thought was a quiet room painted blue with a hint of violet towards the door that seemed to know you—a door that opens slightly, when you want it to, and maybe a window view gives an occasional glimpse of St. Bonnie or St. Clyde sitting in commerce with Bernadette or the Holy Ghost, though goodness knows you wouldn't see him, three sheets to the wind of God.

Goodness knows what led me to pull my heart out like a weed. The straight and narrow is buried somewhere inside me, parallel to my heart, in the shape of a tiny casket.

## Flash Poems

Two metaphors come to mind for the flash poem—a sudden flash of light or of lightning to illuminate a moment that is here and then suddenly gone, and the news flash. The first metaphor speaks to the flash poem's suddenness, generated by its brevity but also frequently achieved by a quick change of direction to create surprise. The second metaphor speaks to the fact that these short poems may be written in fairly flat prose and that the narrative usually speaks with an air of legitimacy or authenticity that both introduces and utilizes urgency. In this way these poems function as a snapshot and leave some indelible image that will resonate with the reader long after the initial reading. Rather than describe how the poems in this section achieve their effects, we leave them to you simply to experience.

## Gary Young

[untitled]

Two girls were struck by lightning at the harbor mouth. An orange flame lifted them up and laid them down again. Their thin suits had been melted away. It's a miracle they survived. It's a miracle they were ever born at all.

## Ben Miller

### #608

Peeping Tom gets a good long look at himself in the mirrored window installed by the widow who has had enough.

**Sean Thomas Dougherty**

## Corpse

The dead dream my eyelids are fields of poppies, a bent-backed farmer with a straw in his mouth walking home through the dust-tinged fields of late summer; beneath the vaulted ceiling Galileo sketched, the dead follow, ant-like, single file, singing.

**Janet Kaplan**

## Little Theory

A machine named Universe knew about itself what it knew at present, nothing more. Away it skipped, blowing bubbles and careful not to step on Father's clock.

## PF Potvin

Mapuche Ranger

When I asked to click a picture of him with the Patagonias in the background he refused. From that perspective he was invisible.

**Bob Heman**

## Information

The boat is the story the ocean tells. The village listens intently and sings for fish. The road carries the carts in only one direction. Where it ends the railroad seems propelled by lights.

*

## Information

The edge of night is propped up against the farm. The chickens are filled with a secret storm. Only the valiant lady is allowed to rest. Soon she will begin a search for tomorrow. Her guiding light is a man filled with wheat.

*

## Information

The beards get on the train and remove their hats. Or they don't remove their hats but instead open their books. Inside their books there are no boats. The women are all modest. In one, a rooster crows.

## Joe Brainard

History

With history piling up so fast, almost every day is the anniversary of something awful.

## Aphorism

An aphorism is a statement, often laconic or clever, that attempts to reveal a personal or universal truth, an acute observation, or a moral commentary. The term was first applied in relation to the aphorisms of Hippocrates and was later distinguished by various writers from Erasmus of Rotterdam to Friedrich Nietzsche. The aphorism generally takes the form of a brief observation that carries a submerged revelation of sorts.

In James Richardson's poem "Vectors" we see a sequence of pieces that apply the principle in both the conventional and the unconventional sense. While many of the poems read like sage fragments espousing fortune cookie wisdom, others seem to spring from the initial observation with intuitive leaps of imagination. Milton Kessler's "Selected Random Sayings by Kosho Shimizu, Chief Abbot, Todaiji" weaves seemingly isolated lines together into a suggestive portrait. The thirty-eight pieces that are taken from Jaime Sabines' "Lost Birds" comprise a much more ambitious sequence. Like Kessler's work, Sabines strings together his aphorisms into a collection that seems to move toward a common objective, though the pieces themselves have little in common with one another aside from the use of apparent contradictions to arrive at subjective truths. Lastly, in the poems taken from "Aerolites," Carlos Edmundo de Ory creates a virtual tapestry of aphorisms. The many individual pieces strung together here like movie stills seem to ebb and flow together not so much for the collective good but as individual truths held momentarily within the same frame.

## James Richardson

### Vectors

7.
Ah, what can fill the heart? But then, what can't?

8.
Shadows are harshest when there is only one lamp.

9.
Desire's most seductive promise is not pleasure but change, not that you might possess your object but that you might become the one who belongs with it.

10.
I say nothing works any more, but I get up and it's tomorrow.

11.
A beginning ends what an end begins.

12.
I walk up the drive for the morning paper and find myself musing, as if the news were fiction. Marvelous that they think of all this, so deadpan strange. Nothing is so improbable as the truth. If the day's headlines hadn't already happened, they would not happen.

13.
Gravity's reciprocal: The planet rises to the sparrow's landing.

14.
When a jet flies low overhead, every glass in the cupboard sings. Feelings are like that: choral, not single; mixed, never pure. The

sentimentalist may want to deny the sadness or boredom in his happiness, or the freedom that lightens even the worst loss. The moralist will resist his faint complicity. The sophisticate, dreading to be found naïve, will exclaim upon the traces of vanity or lust in any motive, as if they were the whole. Each is selling himself simplicity; each is weakened with his fear of weakness.

15.
Road: what the man of two minds travels between them.

16.
The cynic suffers the form of faith without its love. Incredulity is his piety.

17.
Pessimists live in fear of their hope, optimists in fear of their fear.

18.
Writer: how books read each other.

19.
Some people live in a continual state of skepticism and annoyance that they cultivate as a kind of worldly wisdom and are always recruiting for. Let the sun come up and they will roll their eyes, Wouldn't you know it? Profess to be content and they will be disappointed that you have sold your soul for trifles. They wait, hurt and righteous, for the world to prove it really loves them.

20.
If the couple could see themselves twenty years later, they might not recognize their love, but they would recognize their argument.

21.
Each lock makes two prisons.

22.
Painting high on the house. Yellow jackets swarmed around me. I couldn't convince them I was harmless, so I had to kill them.

23.
All stones are broken stones.

24.
Of all the ways to avoid living, perfect discipline is the most admired.

25.
Why would we write if we'd already heard what we wanted to hear?

**Milton Kessler and Tateo Imamura, trs.**

Selected Random Sayings by Kosho Shimizu, Chief Abbot, Todaiji

Flesh deepens spirit. Spirit stings flesh.

Freedom? Try walking.

The dissatisfactions of a happy man, what's more difficult?

Mud on your hands? Sit. Eat.

Don't fight it.

Gold is gold. Silver is silver. Lead is lead.

Cedars in a mountain. Sweetfish in a brook.

Saying anything perfectly? Impossible.

Straight searching is good. Loitering on the way is fragrant.

You have to forgive me.

Once you realize it, it's simple.

There are good days and there are fair days.

A good good, lucky one. A lucky, good good one.

See, even in me there is something good.

To exist is very strange.

Stepping down, be careful, know yourself.

We have been thinking this or that for ten thousand years.

Today is best.

He complains, and enjoys the sound.

## Jaime Sabines

from *Like Lost Birds*

I.
The song isn't the singing. Even the dumb know the singing.

II.
Did you think you could cheat your fate? The sea spits up those who drown before their time. Death won't open its doors until the right moment.

Your corpse has to catch up with you. There's no need to be careful.

III.
I'm hungry. It's time for me to fast.

IV.
I don't wish you anything in the future. I wish that you make for yourself a happy past.

V.
Love is a well-mannered memory (or a persistent forgetting).

XII.
God's secret:
          he brought his lips close to my ear
and didn't say a thing.

XIII.
You won't see anything through the keyhole of a dark room. Knock down the door!

XIV.
The sting of the butterfly is more dangerous by far than the viper's.

XV.
How do you spell water? It should be spelled whater, waahder. Like someone with a great thirst.

XVI.
I'm tired of the poets and the debutantes. They're always rehearsing their first waltz before society.

XVII.
The mouse remained in its hole: I don't mind eating wheat, breadcrumbs and grains of rice. What I can't stand in the world is this oppression, and this darkness.

XVIII.
The perfect crime would be a suicide that looked like a murder. (I ought to put a bullet in my back one of these days.)

XIX.
Since there are now neither teachers nor students, the student asked the wall: what is wisdom? And the wall became transparent.

XXIV.
The young revolutionary artist wants, with all his soul, to shock the bourgeoisie.

The young revolutionary artist lives perpetually shocked by the bourgeoisie.

XXVI.
One by one, he removed the layers of the onion, saying: I've got to find the real onion, I've just got to!

XXX.
Worse than sad is dirty. Poverty dirties the house, the bed, the body and the soul. It chokes on its own vomit, revives only to suffer.

XXXI.
I should have found you ten years earlier, or ten years later. But you had to arrive on time.

XXXII.
I removed my shoes to walk over hot coals.
I removed my skin to take you in.
I removed my body to love you.
I removed my soul to be you.

XXXV.
Today's pastoral poetry can come only from the fields of Vietnam.

XXXVI.
The police burst into the house and caught the partygoers. They hauled them off to jail for being lecherous and perverted. It's only natural. The police can't burst into the street and put an end to other scandals, such as poverty.

XXXVII.
What is the difference between the two or three days of the fly and the two-hundred years of the turtle?

*translated by Philip Pardi*

## Carlos Edmundo de Ory

from *Aerolites*

A poet can never answer anything. He is the sphinx. He asks questions.

Sometimes inspiration lasts the time it takes a mouse to cross the open space between two pieces of furniture.

Why not live with me as if we were angels?

Lunatics are crazy in both legs, poets only crazy in one.

Pillows are the flutes of sleep.

A poem like a newborn's cry.

Frankness as a poetic technique.

I have seen ants. I am ants.

Birds are perfected thoughts.

The imagination, that infinite sponge.

When I was young, cats would come towards me from the horizon. Today cats flee from me, the same ones.

A cadaver factory. Today there are experts who can tell true ones from fabricated ones.

What we call "Mystery" is the closed door of the limit of thought. Those that know the most have seen the door. No one has opened it and gone through.

With curious hands I touch the insect of the unknown.

When you're asleep don't forget to wake up.

A man approached Diogenes and said, "I finally found you!" Diogenes asked him, "And what were you looking for?" The man answered, "I've been wandering around looking for a lantern."

Gold is the refuse of the sun.

Hands are the eyes of the heart.

The black trees of my spirit.

The hand has five fingers—why?

The dead—how they waste time!

The poet is the rooster of twilight.

What does Hell's flag look like?

He was so pessimistic he even believed in God.

It's obvious that man is a microbe.

All pain is real.

Thanatos, an expert in the art of mowing.

Ask a gardener if he ever sees black blossoms.

Raining and weeping are synonymous.

The dead smile at us from their tombs when we visit.

In the United States there are clinics for shy people.

There's nothing more universal than stupidity.

The moon has been popular since the beginning of the world.

Matthew 10:30: "But the very hairs of your head are all numbered." It doesn't mention bald people.

Scottish proverb: "Even if a pig flies it's still not a bird."

Mallarmé was called a terrorist of conjunctions.

Babylonian ruins. Inscription left on a clay tablet: "Look around you, you'll see that all men are imbeciles."

Never forget the lessons of heretics and iconoclasts.

To whom are the insane praying?

Among fruits I admire the banana and the fig.

A truth from Aristotle: "Poets lie a lot."

The Kaballah calls the Earth "the Divine Bride."

"Do what thou wilt" (Plautus)—"What you're doing isn't what you think you're doing" (Antonio Porchia).

They asked Gurdjieff, "Master, what is the difference between East and West?" He responded, "Same shit, different smell."

Before Marinetti decided to call his avant-garde movement Futurism, he thought about calling it Electricism.

I don't trust men who don't laugh.

Has any tyrant in history, fed up with crimes, apologized to humanity?

Nightmares are the nails on the fingers of sleep.

In the book of the mouth, the smile has its own chapter.

Charlemagne didn't even know how to write his name.

The wind is God dancing by.

There's nothing happier than a poor stone.

*translated by Steven J. Stewart*

## List Poems

The list poem may seem specifically tailored to the prose poem but its history can be traced back to ancient oral traditions. Parts of Homer's epics employ the list, and the Christian church made use of the form in litany.

The strategy of the list poem is to catalog a number of entries in response to a theme or prompt. Of course the poet can choose to veer away from that list at anytime, often taking the reader on a surprising path of twists and turns. The success of the list poem, as with any poem, lies in the poet's ability to fully realize the potential of the form and use the reader's expectation to the poem's advantage, frequently by frustrating or diverting from those expectations.

Approaches to the list poem are as varied as the subjects found in the poems themselves. Denise Duhamel uses her list as a platform for meditation. Her *Mille et un sentiments,* excerpted here, follows the meanderings of a stream of consciousness riffing on what "I feel." Joe Brainard's "I Remember," one of the most famous list poems, begins each sentence with the title words, collecting memories into a kind of linguistic photo album. Like Duhamel and Brainard, Andy Brown also uses a repeated phrase (a device known as *anaphora*) to begin each line, in this case building into a kind of secular litany. The poems of Edward Bartók-Baratta and Paul Hoover approach the list differently, using fractured images to cobble loosely together a story that resonates not only from what is said but what is left just out of sight. Carol Bardoff uses a similar technique but chooses to bring her poem full circle to a conclusion that both achieves closure and haunts the reader. Finally, James Tate uses the list as a kind of lullaby to lull the reader into slipping into the comforts of expectation. Of course, nothing can ever be assumed or taken for granted in a Tate poem, especially the credulity of the speaker, as shown by the absurd and absurdly hilarious ending to his "The List of Famous Hats."

## Denise Duhamel

from *Mille et un sentiments*

401. I feel open to writing in general.
402. I feel open to free writing, sestinas, and haiku.
403. I feel open to sonnets and canzones, villanelles and pantoums.
404. I feel open to collages and centos.
405. I feel open to memory and my dreams.
406. I feel open to recipes and headlines and found poems of all kinds.
407. I feel open to nonsense and I feel open to sense.
408. I feel open to I feel open to lists and inversions.
409. I feel open to squirting KY Jelly on my brain, if necessary, to get things going.
410. I feel open to reading the slaves.
411. I feel open to reading the masters.
412. I feel open to taking long walks and clustering.
413. I feel open to taking a nap to see what happens.
414. I feel open to mopping the floor, to see if the gray dreadlocks in soapy water remind me of Ophelia.
415. I feel open to revision and revisionist myth-making.
416. I feel open to bribing the Muse.
417. I feel open to begging.
418. I feel open to melodrama and understatement.
419. I feel open to calling a friend and asking for advice.
420. I feel open to collaboration with children or adults.
421. I feel open to sulking.
422. I feel open to silk worms, the way they create no matter what.
423. I feel open to painting, knitting, making a cake.
424. I feel open to making anything at all.

425. I feel open to humiliation.

426. I feel like opening the dictionary just to look at some words: galaxy, cucumber, scissors, tintinnabulation.

427. I feel open to using these four words in a four line stanza:

> the cucumber peel in the sink was the first tipoff
> that something was wrong—
> then the terrible tintinnabulation of the galaxy
> like scissors preening the fur of a small dog….

428. I feel open to poems within poems.

429. I feel open to giving away my secrets.

430. I feel open to looking like a fool.

431. I feel open to crumpling up what I've written.

432. I feel open to starting all over again.

433. I feel open to free fall and thudding.

434. I feel open to soaring.

435. I feel open to simile and metaphor.

436. I feel open to synecdoche, synesthesia, and sin.

437. I feel open to miracles and mariachi.

438. I feel open to machismo, Mary Poppins, Milk Duds and murder.

439. In other words, I feel open to alliteration.

440. I feel open to assonance as well.

441. I feel open to acting like an absolute ass.

442. I feel open to riding the back of an ass, if I can somehow get a poem out of it.

443. I feel open to sitting on my ass in front of the TV with the sound off to see if that sets off any sparks.

444. I feel open to writing about asses and their different shapes.

445. I feel open to my own desperation for new subject matter.

446. I feel open to the fact that maybe there are already enough poems in the world.

447. I feel open to becoming a train conductor.

448. I feel open to specializing in yoga or suntans.

449. I feel open to getting out of my own head and learning to kickbox.
450. I feel open to going back to the Warhol museum in Pittsburgh to see the punching bags Warhol made with Basquiat.
451. I feel open to punching bags decorated with the face of Christ.
452. I feel open to punching god just to see what it feels like.
453. I feel open to taboo.
454. I feel open to the international sign for toilets in Spain—a stick figure sitting on the can.
455. I feel open to being discreet.
456. I feel open to other international signs for toilets, the silhouette of a woman in a skirt or a man in pants.
457. I feel open to making a Play Doh Garcia Lorca.
458. I feel open to doing Pablo Neruda's Etch a Sketch portrait.
459. I feel open to writing Sylvia Plath's name on a Lite Brite board.
460. I feel open to cartwheels and Scrabble.
461. I feel open to using all the words from a finished Scrabble game in a poem.
462. I feel open to writing a poem using only words from the Official Scrabble Dictionary.
463. I feel open to rigor.
464. I feel open to cheating.
465. I feel open to misinterpretation and mistakes.
466. I feel open to the tee shirt in Miami promoting the Pope's visit. Instead of "I saw the Pope" (el Papa), the shirt read "I Saw the Potato" (la papa).
467. I feel open to seeing the Potato.
468. I feel open to the Holy Potato and its Holy Eyes.
469. I feel open to Mr. Potato Head dressed in a pope's gown.
470. I feel open to Mr. Potato Pope and his views on abortion.
471. I feel open to Pope Potato the Second.

472. I feel open to La Papa Segunda.
473. I feel open to as many languages as possible.
474. I feel open to translation.
475. I feel open to poems of political protest.
476. I feel open to prose poems and open to stanzas.
477. I feel open to couplets about chicken cutlets.
478. I feel open to terza rima about tiramisu.
479. I feel open to anecdotal poems about childhood.
480. I feel open to putting the names of poems in spell-check just to see what alternatives pop up.
481. I feel open to Dorianne Laux becoming Darwin Lax.
482. I feel open to Ai becoming Ax.
483. I feel open to Elizabeth Bishop, Molly Peacock, and Jean Valentine passing through spell-check unaltered.
484. I feel open to caesura. I feel open to lines that bleed into the next.
485. I feel open to meter and counterpoint.
486. I feel open to landscape poems with sheep dots and goat spots and mountains that look like sleeping giants in profile.
487. I feel open to the small white milk teeth of first-graders and mentioning them in poems for good luck.
488. I feel open to mushrooms and mushroom clouds.
489. I feel open to clouds of smoke, clouds of dust, and clouds of pink cotton candy fuzz.
490. I feel open to ritual and magic.
491. I feel open to abstraction and the five senses.
492. I feel open to Mad Libs and liberation of all kinds.
493. I feel open to turning Oscar Wilde's famous quote into a Luscerean word square:

    All bad poetry springs from genuine feeling.
    All bad feelings spring from genuine poetry.
    All genuine poetry springs from bad feelings.
    All genuine feeling springs from bad poetry, etc.

494. I feel open to how the word look looks like "look," the two o's, two round open eyes.
495. I feel open to becoming a nonce word.
496. I feel open to my own goose bumps.
497. I feel open to the little stuck-up hairs on my arm.
498. I feel open to pushing an idea too far.
499. I feel open to holding back.
500. I feel open to closure and the lack of it.

**Edward Bartók-Baratta**

## Will of God

A balloon reaching for the altitude at which explosions occur. An aerial photograph of a field taken by brushfire. The pollen, a spore from Texas, which genetically alters corn in Mexico. Potatoes planted in steps on the sunny side of a cold mountain. A person inside a drum, in a room beneath the bass report of footsteps, the talking of God. The thunder, the lightning, the face lit for a second and is gone. The face followed by another face, the faces in a crowd, they bleed, they weep. The history of faces, their relationship to boots, to razor wire. The thud thud of boots, of faces being delivered to fire. The razor a man drags across his face successfully avoiding his eyes. The drapes behind which mother died. The eyes of poor Oedipus, first one then the other. Tremendous accomplishments, Father hanging himself from a beam in the barn. Mother's clotheslines cut in two, the question of what to do with the other half. Overcooked meat, uncooked meat, the living cow, whether to eat the cloned cattle. Each chicken protected from each chicken, the millions of chickens without beaks. A heat-seeking missile. A one-hundred-percent artificial heart.

## James Tate

### The List of Famous Hats

Napoleon's hat is an obvious choice I guess to list as a famous hat, but that's not the hat I have in mind. That was his hat for show. I am thinking of his private bathing cap, which in all honesty wasn't much different than the one any jerk might buy at a corner drugstore now, except for two minor eccentricities. The first one isn't even funny: Simply it was a white rubber bathing cap, but too small. Napoleon led such a hectic life ever since his childhood, even farther back than that, that he never had a chance to buy a new bathing cap and still as a grown-up—well, he didn't really grow that much, but his head did: He was a pinhead at birth, and he used, until his death really, the same little tiny bathing cap that he was born in, and this meant that later it was very painful to him and gave him headaches, as if he needed more. So, he had to Vaseline his skull like crazy to even get the thing on. The second eccentricity was that it was a *tricorn* bathing cap. Scholars like to make a lot out of this, and it would be easy to do. My theory is simple-minded to be sure: that beneath his public head there was another head and it was a pyramid or something.

**Carol Bardoff**

## 1762

Dawn stuns the fields and forests like a great sudden sunflower.

Toothless and short of breath, an old woman creaks out of bed, bows her head towards a cross on the wall, and begins to pray.

A well-dressed young man on a balcony overlooking his father's cotton crop eyes the sun's halo and wonders how soon it might rain.

A man the same age makes his way between the furry white rows, despairing of his baby boy's future.

In the fifth hut down, that baby boy cries.

When his mother hears him on her way back from the well, she sets her bucket down and lets her spent body fall against a stout tree. But her swollen, dripping breasts will not let her linger.

Captain's orders pound the one good ear of a sailor wrestling a rope freshly soiled with his heavings of last night's rum on a schooner setting sail from Boston harbor.

Half a mile away, a banker grunts at his newspaper, oblivious to the sunlight piercing his bone china cup and to the exotic vapors escaping the teapot before him.

A girl of thirteen lies under a buckskin, lost in a dream of the pale hairy man who frightened her almost two moons ago as she and her sister gathered nuts in the grove.

A seamstress stands at the hearth pouring cornmeal into a pot of boiling water. She can hear her son outside splitting elm logs and coughing from a place deep in his chest.

Ignoring his bride's plea to stay in bed, a preacher holds his breath as he rushes to his ink and pen, fearful that the sermon he has just received be taken back by the same grace which bestowed it.

A hunter drags a limp, bloody elk across a clearing.

A woman checks her undergarment for blood, her jaw clenched with dread, then hearing her husband at the door, gets busy dressing.

Six members of a family silently load their belongings onto a small open wagon.

A four-year-old child shivers and dozes in his sopping bed linens.

Setting down his shovel, a backcountry squatter begins to sing an old German hymn over the bodies of his wife and their newborn daughter.

A schoolteacher sits at her mirror unbraiding her thick red hair and musing on her stomach's noisy rumblings.

The brother of the well-dressed young man steps out from the seventh hut down, his trousers half-buttoned, picturing how it might be different with a white girl.

## Paul Hoover

### The Dog

They were given the dog. The next day it died of a heart attack. The father thought, "At twenty years of age, a dog is rarely playful, but exceptions make the rule." They buried the dog in the yard, and that was that, except for the smell in the room, like that of an older man. There had been the burning dog beside the swimming pool (this was in a dream), the blond dog with blue eyes, the dog in present tense, and the dog in the back of your head. Consciousness is not disjunct, and one thing follows another. An orange was on the table, sliced into equal parts. The father was reading the paper. The mother was humming an old rock song. The children were in their rooms. The dog was climbing the stairs.

**Andy Brown**

## Audubon Becomes Obsessed with Birds

because, as a prelude to mating, the male brings home a gift of
food and sings;
because both birds & whales sing;
because both birds & whales migrate—*ergo* birds are the souls of
whales;
because you need a compass and a map to migrate accurately;
because migrating birds have both;
because the ancient mariners learned to navigate from birds;
because steamer duck, penguins, ratites and emus, ostriches, rheas,
cassowaries and kiwis, Galapagos cormorants and a grebe
from Andean lakes are all truly grounded;
because the New Zealand Takahe, the Mesites, the Rails and the
Kagu cannot take off either;
because the Dodo, the Mascarene Solitaire, the Great Auk and the
Elephant-bird might still exist today, if only they had flown;
because the Romans tagged their legs with coloured rags to tell
the folks at home the name of He who won the chariot race;
because Greek sages practiced divination from the flight of birds;
because the Rongorongo tablets of Easter island tell of *The Rite of
The Sacred Birdman;*
because the scribes of ancient Egypt saw existence rise from Non-
Existence in the shape of the *Bennu Bird;*
because the *Bennu Bird* becomes the *Phoenix* of the Greeks;
because the Phoenix builds a nest of scented branches, starts a fire
and is consumes by flames;
because the Romans saw *Aquarius* as a heaven-flying bird;
because the Maya saw *Aquarius* as *Coz*, the *Celestial Falcon*;
because the ancient Hindus called *Aquarius* "*Garuda*," the
Birdman; vehicle of Vishnu, the *Preserver*;

because these myths mix birds, astronomy and water into symbols
of rebirth and life;
because birds know what time it is;
because vultures gathering indicate dead men;
because birds are like ideas—they visit us fleetingly, then
disappear

## Joe Brainard

from *I Remember*

I remember when I thought that if you did anything bad, policemen would put you in jail.

I remember one very cold and black night on the beach alone with Frank O'Hara. He ran into the ocean naked and it scared me to death.

I remember lightning.

I remember wild red poppies in Italy.

I remember selling blood every three months on Second Avenue.

I remember a boy I once made love with and after it was all over he asked me if I believed in God.

I remember when I thought that anything old was very valuable.

I remember *Black Beauty.*

I remember when I thought that Betty Grable was beautiful.

I remember when I thought I was a great artist.

I remember when I wanted to be rich and famous. (And I still do!)

## Repetition

The recurrence of a word, phrase, or sound in a poem adds emphasis to that word, phrase, or sound while establishing, as in music, a pattern that the reader comes to anticipate. This anticipation can be further reinforced with recurrences or can be frustrated by the word's or sound's sudden absence. Obviously, repetition is an important tool in some of the other strategies presented in this book, most notably in some List poems.

Juliana Leslie's poem "Idyll" and Milton Kessler's "Comma of God" both have a meditative take on the use of repetition. While Leslie's poem subtly changes the words that are repeated as the poem progresses, Kessler's poem begins each line of the poem "I am nothing compared to…." Both poems lull the reader before leaping to new lines that change the context, constantly breathing new life and relevance into the lines. While the Kessler poem would fit nicely into the List Poem section, the Leslie poem begins as though it might be a list poem, but deftly changes direction; that change of direction is then established as a new pattern in the poem.

The poems of Charles Kesler and David Ignatow take a more narrative approach; their repeated phrases intersperse throughout the poems but not with the regularity of the previous two poems. In Kesler's "A Traveling Monk Observes," the repeated line "I have noticed in my travels that people…" leads the speaker on a train of thought that baffles him until, at the poem's end, he arrives at an ironic epiphany that casts all previous observations in a new light. David Ignatow's poem "The Story of Progress" uses the repetition of the phrase "for me" in a context that evolves from clever to profound in the speaker's gradual understanding of identity and self.

The repetitions of G. C. Waldrep's "Who Is Josquin des Prez?" become a kind of linguistic dance, not unlike the musical steps of Gertrude Stein in their associative leaps, but perhaps with a more readily recognizable narrative reference point. The musical effect of the repetitions here are similar to the effect of the rondeau, a form of verse derived from a medieval dance. Brian Clements's "Basket of Brains" repeats Kant's question "What is enlightenment?" and repeats several other words for emphasis and irony, but also is built around a repetitive rhythm similar to the rhythm of "The House that Jack Built." Matthew Cooperman's "It Is Absence..." repeats the phrase "There are certain patterns of experience known as habits," but also employs a subtler repetition of similar sentence structures—look out for them as you read the poem.

## Juliana Leslie

### Idyll

You will need a canvas and a body to move with.

You will need to paint a surface tension and call it lemon.

You will need a real garden and many creatures and many earthlings.

This will become the movement of two or more bodies finding themselves at home in each other's horizon.

This is the world of earth and earthworm.

This is liquid meaning we are made of water because water passes through us.

This is language meaning something sea level or something turbulent.

Or a place under the sun notwithstanding.

This is the cruel drama in the life of the delicate flower.

Choose yourself any shape and color. Choose elsewhere choose azure choose midnight.

Choose to say buoyant or divine grace or catastrophe. Choose the charming form of a tree.

Choose a texture both expansive and dynamic.

Choose a flock of pigeons and call them otherworldly.

## Milton Kessler

### Comma of God

I am nothing compared to the Medicaid sneer
I am nothing compared to the owner of the door
I am nothing compared to the elevator of Heidegger
I am nothing compared to the spokes of Vincent's Belgian sunflower
I am nothing compared to Rodin's least mistress
I am nothing compared to the frames of Hamlet
I am nothing compared to a critic or chauffeur
I am nothing compared to my old fire engine
I am nothing compared to the breasts I see
I am nothing compared to a tree in any season
I am nothing compared to the escalator of Duchamp
I am nothing compared to Marinetti's future
I am nothing to compare with Turner's clouds
I am nothing to compare with the lens of Claude
I am nothing to compare with my mother in 1930
I am nothing to compare with the cockroach in the drain
I am nothing to compare to the jew-hater's snot
I am nothing compared to the beak or the bill
I am nothing compared to the past or the present
I am nothing to compare with any suit on the rack
I am nothing to compare to a loaf or child
I am nothing to compare with any syllable of Homer
I am nothing to compare with the foot of a chair
I am nothing to compare with the truth of your anger
I am nothing compared with what I failed to do
I am nothing compared with one note of Lester Young
I am nothing compared to the images of Vietnam
I am nothing compared to the furnace of Dresden

I am nothing compared to the last drops of snow
I am nothing compared to a bicycle with wings
I am nothing compared to the comma of God

## Charles Kesler

### A Traveling Monk Observes

I have noticed in my travels that people do not put Kleenex out for guests. They do not even put out trash cans to put the Kleenex in that they do not put out. I have noticed in my travels that people do not put towels in their restrooms for their guests to wipe their hands on after they wash their hands. I have spent much time meditating on why this is so as I have waited for my hands to dry, usually in a dog paddling or bicycle tire pumping manner. I confess I sometimes discretely use their decorative towels to wipe my hands on, but I always feel guilty and end up rolling around on the floor asking the host to please forgive me. About half of the hosts do forgive me and the other half usually include the shell in the scrambled eggs they cook for me at breakfast. I crunch and smile and determine to mend my ways, but decorative towels loved this much make me want to puke on them, but I don't like to get sick so I'll just go on meditating while my hands dry. I have noticed in my travels that people do not put a lamp near enough to the guest bed if at all. Aha I see now. I do not need a Kleenex, a trash can, a hand towel, or a lamp because I am A Traveling Monk and I meditate, I meditate, I meditate, and I meditate in the dark.

## David Ignatow

### The Story of Progress

The apple I held and bit into was for me. The friend who spoke to me was for me. My father and mother were for me. The little girl with brown hair and brown eyes who looked and smiled shyly and ran away was for me, although I never dared follow her because I feared she would not understand that she was for me alone.

The bed I slept in was for me. The clothes I wore were for me. The kindness I showed a dead bird one winter by placing it in my warm pocket was for me. The time I went to the rescue of my sister from a bully was to prove myself, for me. The music on the radio, the books I was beginning to read, all were for me.

I had hold of a good thing, me, and I was going to give of my contentment to others, for me, and when I gave, it was taken with a smile that I recognized as mine, when I would be given. I had found that for me was everybody's way, and I became anxious and uncertain. I held back a bit when I exchanged post card pictures of baseball players, with a close look at what I was getting in return to make sure I was getting what I could like, and when my parent bought me a new pair of gloves after I had lost the first pair I was sure that for me was not as pure in feeling as the first time, because I was very sorry that my parents had to spend an extra dollar to replace my lost gloves, and so when I looked up at the night stars, for me remained silent, and when my grandmother died, for me became a little boy sent on an errand of candles to place at the foot and head of her coffin.

## G. C. Waldrep

### Who Is Josquin des Prez?

A little winter, a drop at winter, a descent and then a steeper dwindling in the depths of winter, a snowdrop. A small sketch. A snowdrop signals the end of one thing and the beginning of another, a wider imprecation. How do you do. How does one do. A snowdrop reminds.

To begin. There is a market, there is buying and selling, there is that proverbial marrying and being given in marriage as one joins another. And suits this action, as from field, as from the space defined within a field, as from a white flag. Sixteen cents allowing for the anachronism which is a necessary liberty as with marriage as with may I hold you, may I kiss your lips, may I move my hand between your cheek and neck, between your necks and the basin of your shoulders. May I purchase this felt hat. Yes thank you.

In the road they were married and marrying. In the mud and dung which were frozen it being winter, or almost winter, or barely yet winter signaling outward to some different season. Some on horseback, some on foot. They were not thinking of dying. They were trading places with the dead, this is continual, this from moment to moment is what we call life. Some were some were not thing of money. Some were not thinking of sleep.

What is sleep. Sleep is the penetration of value by a perfect means.

In any resurrection there may be doubts, there may be misgivings, there may well be interruptions, there may be the confidence of a period style. There may be distortion this may be one aim. Any performance is a rondeau and so not drawn from legacy. Any performance is provisional, as pence for francs or dollars for rubles. (See What is ballet.)

If one cannot imagine a snowdrop then one might imagine its absence. A snowdrop as its own absence, a snowdrop is its own absence, a snowdrop absent. A snowdrop. White on white/on white.

## Matthew Cooperman

### It is Absence We Cultivate Knowing the Corpse

There are certain patterns of experience known as habits. There are certain patterns of experience known as habits. Collecting the Days could be construed as a productive use of Time. For what is this thing called World? We discuss the urgings of "frame" but where from?

I mean what is this thing called Heaven and how can I help my Family? Who at the agency keeps capitalizing my Principle? The concept of daze obtrudes as the obvious hour. It is *there,* as are you, the voice still quiet beauty inside my head.

Emerson says "Our faith comes in moments, our vice is habitual." So another version of bewilderment, moving from person to labor. There are certain patterns of experience known as habits. The wild of bees, the swerve of men.

From the beginning the sky tribe, the astral Riviera. But the rapid development of mines, the corruption of language to cut the daisy stem. When a flower looms it is showing the height of despair, the tiny eyes with which we see undersides life.

Now who is Al-Fasoud and where is my ladder of light?

All of this sounds like America, free and discursive. We discuss the urgings of "frame" and try to believe in words. The pace is relentless and troubles the natives. A confusion arises between subjectivity and subjectivism, the inevitability of the former in a day of shopping, and the philosophical problem of the latter in the privilege of a well-chosen birth. To say there is a rhythm to this madness?

Your panel sounds interesting and I'm certainly amenable to its thinking. I work a lot in the "divide" and there's a commitment here to play. That is, the distinction between the Beautiful and the

Useful is a false dichotomy such that a person is always *for* something. Such suasion needs a house, a "how does it work."

Everyone grapples with the question of where they are. There's a way in which boredom forces the issue. You can say you're on break, but the planet differs. Drift, gaze, smoke, digress, where to live in a body not really yours? It is absence we cultivate knowing the corpse. I think of him as an envelope steamed open by war.

There's a faith in assuming the book but it don't mean a thing if it ain't got others. I mean what is this thing called Heaven and how can I help my Family? As Howe says, "Access to the metaphysical is a requirement of need." Be brave enough to kill your selves. Our vice comes in moments and out faith is habitual.

## Brian Clements

### Basket of Brains

What, you might ask, is enlightenment? Does it happen in the brain? Is it a meeting of science and faith or the erasure of both? Let's find out. To start, it might be useful to consider all of the brains in a single group:

By the way the brains of this group, it appears, flash with streetlight, tire-hum, leaf-swell, we know they are attuned to what is outside the window, and that what is outside the window repeats. What repeats contains threads. Threads contain length and breadth, and, twisted, contain period, and length and period make a cycle.

The brain and the rest of the body among the bodies of this group, it appears, are attuned to what is outside the window the way the hearts of the bodies in this group are attuned to bodies returning scarred from the front. In daily language, "hearts" means nearly the same as "stop loss."

A body is a stop loss. In daily language, a stop-lossed loved one is one lost. A stop-lossed loved one, though, knows lost lore—for example, that the brain cannot work without the liver. It is often said of the brain that it will act as the brain that it is, but also it will act as the liver that it is, as the thyroid that it is, as the blood that it is in the bodies of this group.

That is, the mind is a woven thing, woven of the things of the body by spinners, weavers, and dyers born of the brains of the bodies of this group.

What, then, is enlightenment? Is it as predictable, for example, as the heat-woven weather? If weather were predictable, we would capture it. And minds? As bodies are capturable, the brains of the bodies of a group are capturable. And where might we look to capture them?

Here we have Brain at Brain Architects Guild of America, which does not exist. Here we have Brain at Brain Conference Center, Brain at Enlightenment Bar, Brain at Cryogenic Rejuvenation Center, which do not exist.

But here, at last, we have Brain Drives Over Land Mine, Brain Makes Choice Between Eating and Filling Prescription, Brain Says Negotiate (But Means Dictate), Brain Sends Signal to Turn Over Stomach at Unexpected Knock on the Door.

Are these enlightenment? Or is enlightenment Brain Opens Door to New Dimension? Or is it You Are Nothing But a Speck on the Map? Whichever, the brains of the bodies of this group are in the dark, sitting in the dark and spinning, spinning a dark and regular thread in a regular cycle that goes spin, weave, and dye, spin, weave, and dye, spin, weave, and dye.

## Variation on or Development of a Theme

A "theme" in a poem may refer to a controlling or informing idea behind a poem, or it may simply refer to any idea, phrase, or image with enough complexity to resonate in the poem. Variation on the theme can be used as a springboard that ultimately leads to deeper complexity, a fresh perspective of the original premise, or at the very least, an exploration of the richness of language itself.

Gian Lombardo's poem "Devil of a Time" begins with the speaker hypothesizing about the possibility of being attacked by barbarians. If the poem's initial premise seems somewhat lighthearted, then the speaker's rambling narrative compliments it perfectly. Lombardo's deadpan delivery ultimately reverses the initial conflict by speculating the best defense to his hypothetical quandary would be "...being something beside myself," lending the opening gambit greater weight. In the poem "Socrates is a Man," Lewis LaCook builds a poem around a single phrase: "Language is a word..." The phrase is circled and elaborated, allowing the reader to witness firsthand the energy and possibility that can be released from such a seemingly innocuous line by the fertile and imaginative mind of the poet. John Yau takes the point even further in his sequence "Corpse and Mirror." Yau constructs sections that function like vignettes, each linked by the presence of the aforementioned objects but disparate in their context and haunting in their stark details that accumulate into a kind of alternate reality. By contrast, Catherine Bowman's "No Sorry" begins and ends with an old bread knife. In the course of the poem, however, Bowman takes the reader on a dizzying meditation that spans the range of objects humans use to hurt one another from knife, to thermonuclear warheads, to toxin agents. In his poem "The Encyclopedia Britannica Uses Down Syndrome to Define 'Monster,'" Brooke Horvath uses a sequence of anecdotes as variations of counterpoint on our repeated failure to come to terms with real human beings. Richard Garcia's "Chickenhead" uses a simple compare and contrast strategy for its variations.

## Gian Lombardo

### Devil of a Time

Many, many times I've thought about arming myself against barbarians. But I couldn't decide whether a barbarian was someone I wouldn't recognize, or whether it was someone I couldn't understand.

Either way, I believe I'd end up with too many barbarians.

I believe if I need an enemy to protect myself from, it's better to have a particular enemy—one I'd know was a threat.

But if I recognized that threat, wouldn't that be something familiar? I've got the feeling I'd be contravening myself.

In that case, I'd guess I'd have to be out of sorts, being something beside myself.

## Lewis LaCook

### Socrates is a Man

*"Language is a word..."*

Language is a word. The coffee, thick and tart like rain if sex were a kiddie pool, is finally finished and in your hands to warm them up. In the same direction as synchronicity, a car outside turns over as the central air kicks in. It's about that time.

"Language is a word" is a sentence. The central air, black and sour as if rain carried a violin case down Eryk Salvaggio's street, kicks in every window of every abandoned car turning over in the steadily unbruising dawn. Your warm hands gaze longingly out the window. The kiddie pool, having been open all night, finally shuts off on a rush of spastic crinoline jets. In case you were wondering, all women are mortal. The time at the tone will be:

"'Language is a word' is a sentence," she writes, quite pleased with the cleverness with which she has subverted the objecthood of the previous sentence and virtually uttered a novel thought. The rain spoke with a slight lisp, revealing its lower socio-economic origins; it had been promiscuous in its youth, and now, older, had retreated into a well-worn piety that felt like cars turning over and bursting into flame. All the sex in the house has molded, and must be thrown out. That happens in these climes; the children, exhausted after night-swimming until the rim of day, slip back into their caskets, sated until dusk trickles through the hinges again. In case you were wondering, you are now completely out of time. So much space in there I had to stand still.

**John Yau**

## Corpse and Mirror I

2

When one of our citizens dies, his head is cut off and placed inside a mirror-lined box. The box is tightly sealed, allowing no light to enter its interior, and placed inside the least used room of the house. Each night, someone from the family must sleep beside the varnished cube in which the head resides. After two weeks have elapsed, the box can be buried beside the rest of the corpse.

However, if everyone in the family bears a grudge against the deceased, and anger so deep that death has not removed its poison, they may burn the box and joyfully kick the ashes and bone fragments into the river. This decision must be reached without ever being mentioned. Finally, once the ashes begin floating downstream, the deceased's name can never be brought up in conversation again.

Once the head is inside the box, the eyelids will push up against the weight of dreams and sleep until they open. It will never occur to him that his head has been severed from his body. Instead, he will believe he has been kidnapped and buried in the sand. Before him is a road stretching to the horizon. Above him the moon patrols the walls of its vast domain. Escape is impossible. By morning the vultures will begin circling patiently.

Soon he begins rambling, imagining his mouth is parched and full of sand. This is a signal. Whoever is sleeping in the room must awaken immediately and begin listening to the voice echoing inside the box. What happens next depends on who has died. If instructions are uttered, they must be followed faithfully. If a confession is made, it must be heard without judgment. Whatever is said must be kept a secret.

If you are sent to another city, you must saddle your horse at dawn and leave without speaking to anyone. Once you are there, you must find the house the voice described. A house similar to all the houses on all the winding streets in this haphazardly designed city, and yet different in one essential way. When the door opens you will know why. However, if the person who answers the door is puzzled by your request, then you have failed to listen to the instructions carefully enough. Too many words slipped through your excitement. In this case, you must return to your house without speaking to anyone along the way. No one in your family will greet you. You cannot sleep beside the box again, but must remain inside your room until the tow weeks are over.

One night, after the box has been buried or burned, you will hear something outside your window, inside your dream. The words may not be words at all, but the fluttering of a bird caught in a snare. A broken pot. A bucket falling into a well. Listen carefully. He may need to speak to you once again.

## Corpse and Mirror II

1

When a comet passes over the town, whoever sees it knows a corpse will be discovered at the edge of the forest shortly after dawn.

Last week, an old woman, who embroiders tablecloths with human hair, saw one from her kitchen window, and knew her grandson had wandered too far from the road leading home.

Now, whenever she stops to talk to someone, she asks: "Was the message delivered too early? Or remembered too late?"

If they are lying face up with their eyes open and clear, as if they are still puzzled by the last thing they saw, then they must be cremated, their ashes scattered over the lake.

If, however, they are lying facedown with their eyes closed, as if they had dozed off while recalling the intricate lattice of a pleasant hour they passed through years ago, then they must be buried at once. No stone can mark the spot.

Otherwise, both the deceased and its discoverer are doomed to remember a moment, its sunlit basket of fruit, as if each drop of significance will elude them forever.

Some find it impossible to believe their life is chained to a comet. If they were to submit to the possibility the stars have exiled us from their provinces, then they would have to accept that the story unfolds without them.

In the afternoon, you see them huddled in the corners of dark cafes. Sometimes, their mumbling reaches the street the way the sound of dry branches rubbing against each other pierces a dream.

Then one is awakened by a comet passing overhead; and once again the light echoing in our eyes reminds us that we are meant to wander from one day to the next, like dogs without masters.

2

When you break a mirror, you must count up the pieces to see if they are equal to your age. If they are, you must change your name and leave town at once.

Do not speak to anyone you meet on the road until you have reached a town, where everyone speaks a language different from your own. Otherwise, you will wake up in someone else's coffin.

Do not tell anyone your name until you have forgotten every endearment (affectionate or otherwise) you were summoned by as a child. Otherwise, one morning, the only voice you hear will be your own, echoing down the long hallways beneath sleep.

The voice will begin telling you a story about a child who hears someone calling his name. No matter which way the child turned, the source of the voice eluded him. And, as the story enters daylight's tenement, you will realize that you are the child, and it is your voice calling.

## Corpse and Mirror III

1

When the movie ends and the lights come on, the audience is puzzled by the sight of a corpse reclining on a velvet couch in clothes of human hair. Each item has been carefully woven together, so that the hair resembles a white silk shirt and a three-piece wool suit flecked with gold.

On the mahogany table is a brass ashtray in the shape of a bulldog. Smoke curls from its nostrils as if it had swallowed a cigarette. An emerald butterfly glistens on his left index finger. In his bluish gray hands is a book whose pages are made of glass.

The next afternoon I drive to the outskirts of town, where there is a restaurant named after a traitor famous for his ingenious disguises. Many of the patrons think that even the name is a disguise, and that he still moves among us.

I have never been able to remember the plot of the movie, only the colors it traced against the arch of the bridge connecting the room's two halves together. On one side shines the movie and on the other sits the corpse. Passing back and for the between them is a conversation made of human hair.

## 2

When the movie ends, the lights come on. The audience is puzzled by the sight of a large oval mirror leaning awkwardly against a column, which wasn't there at the beginning of the evening's entertainment.

Scarves stop fluttering; and, one by one, hands settle nervously into laps, like birds circling the parameters of their nests. Mouths twist beneath the receding wave of whispers, almost as if there were a place they could hide.

A reflection pierces the mirror, though the stage is empty. The men see a woman brushing her hair, while the women see a man trimming his beard.

Later, no one will be able to agree on what they saw. The memory of one event will twist around the memory of another. All that remains is the ache of trying to recall a moment, whose slanting roof of sunlight has long since fallen in. By then the mirror will have varnished and the movie will have started. This time in pieces.

## Catherine Bowman

### No Sorry

Do you have any scissors I could borrow? *No, I'm sorry I don't.* What about a knife? You got any knives? A good paring knife would do or a simple butcher knife or maybe a cleaver? *No, sorry all I have is this old bread knife my grandfather used to butter his bread with every morning.* Well then, how about a hand drill or hammer, a bike chain, or some barbed wire? You got any rusty razor-edged barbed wire? You got a chain saw? *No, sorry I don't.* Well then maybe you might have some sticks? *I'm sorry, I don't have any sticks.* Well how about a stone tied to a stick? *You mean a club?* Yeah, a club. You got a club? *No, sorry, I don't have any clubs.* What about some fighting picks, war axes, military forks, or tomahawks? *No, sorry, I don't have any kind of war fork, axe, or tomahawk.* What about a morning star? *A morning star?* Yeah, you know, those spiked ball and chains they sell for riot control. *No, nothing like that. Sorry.* Now I know you said you don't have a knife except for that dull old thing your grandfather used to butter his bread with every morning and he passed down to you but I thought maybe you just might have an Australian dagger with a quartz blade and a wood handle, or a bone dagger, or a Bowie, you know it doesn't hurt to ask? Or perhaps one of those lethal multi-purpose stilettos? *No, sorry.* Or maybe you have a simple blow pipe? Or a complex airgun? *No, I don't have a simple blow pipe or a complex airgun.* Well then maybe you have a jungle carbine, a Colt, a revolver, a Ruger, an axis bolt-action repeating rifle with telescopic sight for sniping, a sawed-off shotgun? Or better yet, a gas-operated self-loading fully automatic assault weapon? *No, sorry I don't.* How about a hand grenade? *No.* How about a tank? *No.* Shrapnel? *No.* Napalm? *No.* Napalm 2? *No, sorry I don't.* Let me ask you this. Do you have any intercontinental ballistic missiles? Or submarine launched cruise missiles? Or multiple independently targeted reentry missiles? Or terminally guided anti-tank shells or projectiles? Let me ask you this. Do you have any fission bombs or hydrogen bombs? Do you have any thermonuclear warheads? Got any electronic measures or electronic counter-measures or electronic counter-counter-measures? Got any biological weapons or germ warfare, preferably in aerosol form? Got any enhanced tactical neutron lasers emitting massive doses of whole-body gamma radiation? Wait a minute. Got any plutonium? Got any chemical agents, nerve agents, blister agents, you know, like mustard gas, any choking agents or incapacitating agents or toxin agents? *Well, I'm not sure. What do they look like?* Liquid vapor powder colorless gas. Invisible. *I'm not sure. What do they smell like?* They smell like fruit, garlic, fish or soap, new-mown hay, apple blossoms, or like those little green peppers that your grandfather probably would tend to in his garden every morning after he buttered his bread with that old bread knife that he passed down to you.

## Brooke Horvath

### The Encyclopedia Britannica Uses Down Syndrome to Define "Monster"

I.
The encyclopedia's definition leaves my daughter holding hands with Grendel, the Cyclops, Frankenstein's monster, the mythic deformities of hell.

Chancing upon this definition leaves me face to face with the unspeakable.

II.

She is a monster who cries, recites with her sister the alphabet, has fallen in love with the boy at preschool who opens her yogurt for her.

She is a monster who meets with fear and stares outside and inside, holds the usual human emotions imprisoned by more than usual inarticulateness.

III.

My insurance company will not pay for her therapy. Therapy, a letter tells me, is covered only following an accident.

My insurance company does not believe in genetic accidents. My insurance company covers only human beings.

IV.

The Encyclopedia Britannica, with its assurance that truth is tidy and knowable and human-sized, can shove its learning up its human ass.

It is anything human that is alien to me.

V.

My monster's favorite shirt has four hearts across its front. I ask her why she likes this shirt so much, and she points to the hearts.

You like hearts, I ask. But she shakes her head no, pointing again to each heart in turn and saying carefully: mommy, daddy, sister, me.

## Richard Garcia

### Chickenhead

Chickenhead makes me think of Jesus. Even though Jesus died on the cross for our sins and Chickenhead was just a hood who died hanging from a meat hook. First, take the Romans—Italian, right? In other words, gangsters. Take hanging from a cross and hanging from a meat hook. Both ways, you die slow.

Chickenhead used to shoot the heads off chickens in his backyard when he was a kid. Except, instead of blowing them apart he would put them together.

Chickenhead was a big shot of the block. In more ways that one, since he weighed three hundred pounds. When Chickenhead got in the back of his Cadillac it would tilt to one side. Jesus was big in his neighborhood too. But he was skinny. When Jesus would get on a donkey-maybe it was an old, decrepit, almost dead donkey-that donkey would trot along skimming over stones as if it had wings.

Jesus made people mad. Chickenhead made people mad. Skimming a little off the top is O.K., it's expected. But after Chickenhead bought that second Cadillac and after what he did to that Gypsy girl in the back room of the cleaners with her dad forced to watch, he had to go.

The Romans had dice. We had dice. The Romans had a wooden cross. We had a meat hook. The Romans had spears and vinegar. We had a bucket of cold water and one of those electric cattle pokers.

Chickenhead hung there. We'd give him a splash and an electric goose once in a while. His whole body would shimmer, all blubbery. Took Jesus three hours to die. Took Chickenhead three days.

Jesus got famous. First guy to beat Death at his own game. Nobody remembers Chickenhead but me. And if some stranger, a cop maybe, asked, Did I know Chickenhead? I'd play it safe just like Saint Peter when he hears that cock crow, once, twice, three times, and I'd say, I never knew nobody named Chickenhead.

## Fable

The fable is one of the oldest forms of narrative, and its roots can be traced back to oral story-telling and ancient religious traditions. In the world of prose poetry, the fable is somewhat unique in that it was already a well established and culturally significant genre long before the prose poem came along to breathe new life into it. The fable is generally a short fictitious narrative that often, though not always, personifies animals as the central characters and usually concludes with a cautionary moral. The fable as it is known today is probably most indebted to the tales of the Greek Aesop. In the United States the form was perhaps best realized in the "Trickster Tales" and other fables passed down orally by the various tribes indigenous to North America.

Many of Russell Edson's prose poems take the form of the fable. While Edson frequently use the fabulist practice of making animals the main characters, in his poem "Clouds" the reader finds a married couple atop a roof considering their new perspective and what to do next. It is not until the husband's sexual advances reach their crescendo that the wife looks up and kicks the poem into another orbit by remarking on the clouds. The subject matter may seem unusual, even Surrealistic, but the phrasing, the pacing of dialogue, and the progression strategy that Edson uses are right from the pages of the Fabulist play book. In Arielle Greenberg's "Pastoral," the form of the fable is ultimately used against the reader's expectations. The poem builds steadily towards a climax that is never realized but is instead replaced by a surprising twist that brings the fantasy to a darkly literal level. Andrew Michael Roberts and Jamey Dunham use the fable for ironic commentaries about the contemporary world. Roberts' poem relays the plight of a "superhero" searching for her identity, while Dunham's poem "Urban Myth" follows the trials and tribulations of a couple who have given birth to a lemur. Both poems end with a twist and more than a bit of social satire. The poems by Brian Brennan, James Tate, and W. S. Merwin use the fable in variations on familiar religious tales or parables. John Bradley's poem pretends at first to be a kind of parable, and in fact uses phrasing reminiscent of parables, then takes off on a wild departure. Despite the weight of these themes each is able to render a poem that approaches the subject with a good sense of humor and hints at the deeper implications of what seems to be humorous about them.

**Russell Edson**

## Clouds

A husband and wife climbed to the roof of their house, and each at the extremes of the ridge stood facing the other the while that the clouds took to form and reform.

The husband said, shall we do backward dives, and into windows floating come kissing in a central room?

I am standing on the bottom of an overturned boat, said the wife.

The husband said, shall I somersault along the ridge of the roof and up your legs and through your dress out of the neck of your dress to kiss you?

I am a roof statue on a temple in an archaeologist's dream, said the wife.

The husband said, let us go down now and do what it is to make another come into the world.

Look, said the wife, the eternal clouds.

## Andrew Michael Roberts

### Amnesia

A superhero awakens, lying wounded in the grass in Couch Park, across from the synagogue. She sits up slowly and looks about, puzzled to find her head throbbing, muscles sore, her multicolored spandex suit ripped and stained. She's hungry. She can't remember the last time she ate. Hell, she can't remember anything. How did I get here? I'm a superhero, surely, but which one? What are my special powers?

She limps three blocks to the YWCA. Something to eat. A shower. Maybe some TV in the lounge. Soon she's enrolled in the transitional housing program. She's landing a job in fast food, working hard in brown polyester. She's trainee of the month; her attendance is perfect. She's promoted to management, given first choice on vacation time. Given the circumstances, she's felling pretty good about things.

It's on lunch breaks, though, that she sits alone, flipping through comic books—four or five new ones every week—hoping she'll turn up in the pages, maybe in a scene with Wonder Woman or Green Lantern. And she gets weepy now and then, sipping her chocolate shake, guilt eating her, knowing a train is derailing somewhere, a baby carriage rolling downhill into traffic....

## Arielle Greenberg

### Pastoral

> *Because the Jew and Nature, those are two separate things.*
> *—Paul Celan,*
> *"Conversation in the Mountains"*

This old schlepper, he was hungry. He was always hungry, and he was always broke, and he was stupid as a rock, and everywhere he went he was followed by his only friend, a dirty, scrawny goat. Yes, there are beautiful animals in the world, but this one was no looker, let me tell you. This was a disgusting, revolting old goat, with stink-grass in its teeth, and a long beard that had drool stuck in it, and crooked horns and yellow curling hair around its hooves from where it had stepped in its own pish. And the old man and the goat, for years they were like brothers, laughing, singing, but the man was hungry, he was poor, he had no money. So one day he said Goat, what can I tell you? We've been friends a long time, but I'm hungry. It's time to be eaten. And the goat said, You're crazy in the head. Without me, you have nothing, not a little song to keep you going. No one else to put up with your stupid jokes all the time and your smell. The man said, My smell? and the goat said, Shut up and listen to me. We'll get you a good, fat chicken, and you won't need to eat me. We'll put some butter and salt, make it nice. You'll eat, you'll like. And the man thought it sounded like not such a bad idea, so the two friends went off to find a chicken. Did they know how to find a chicken? No, of course not—they had pebbles for brains, believe me. But they thought, chickens are like birds. We'll listen, see if we can hear a song. And off they went through the forest to hear a chicken song. They went up and down hills, mud all over the place, it was raining, it was misery, let me tell you. Finally there was a song coming out of a tree. All right already, said the goat. I'm starving, said the man. Can I eat it raw? Hey, chicken! Come here! And the song stopped and a songbird stepped out on a little branch and gave the man and the goat such a look. What, are you calling me a chicken? said the songbird. I'm no chicken. I'm dying of no food, said the man. Where's the salt shaker? The bird took a hop back on his branch and said, You're the dumbest shmuck I ever saw. You don't tell an animal you're going to eat it before you eat it. Stupid in the head! Come on, both of you—we'll get a nice cow. I haven't had steak in weeks. And so off they went, three jerks like you couldn't believe, nearly with cramps from the hunger. It was all bushes and thorns and god knows what, some kind of jungle almost, and it was night when the moon shone a light over an enormous milky-white rump. Cow! cried the man in such joy. Go to hell, said the woman, turning around, having just had a little bath in the river. The man looked at her with a crazy eye and said, I have to eat you. I haven't had food in days. I wanted to eat my goat but he's my only companion. I wanted to eat this bird here but he's too smart for me. You're a big juicy girl—you got a fork and knife around here somewhere? The girl said, You can't eat me. I'm the same as you; I'm a person. Persons don't eat persons. It'd be like eating your mother. And the man said, I hope not—she was all dark meat.

## Brian Brennan

### On the Side of the Angels

After the end of the world the angels agree not to mention it for seven years, which isn't easy, having looked after it for so long. Now when they meet each other—and they do, all the time, there's no where else to go—and they ask each other how they are, there's nothing to say, no "Bob Marcus didn't get hit by a truck," or "Elizabeth Prawler had a girl." There are no prayers to answer, no souls to be fought for.

Some of the angels take up pool. Others delve into quantum physics. A couple open a restaurant, and business is great until the other angels catch onto the fact that the food's not so good. Then competition. Stores open and close. There's an angel distribution company, angel truckers and an angel accountant, a whole city of angels with parking spaces and an angel traffic cop.

God figures the end of the world should have solved all this, that now there would be more time to contemplate light and hosanna his general godliness. No such luck. The pool-playing angels take up hustling. There's an angel lawyer, angel rock band, and angel rock promoter. Some angels protest the loss of angel values; others demand better wages.

God turns them all into apes. They pick lice off each other's bodies. Eat grubs. Occasional violence. It's quiet at night. Maybe my mistake was starting with angels, God thinks, and lets evolution take its other, more natural course.

**James Tate**

## Goodtime Jesus

Jesus got up one day a little later than usual. He had been dreaming so deep there was nothing left in his head. What was it? A nightmare, dead bodies walking all around him, eyes rolled back, skin falling off. But he wasn't afraid of that. It was a beautiful day. How 'bout some coffee? Don't mind if I do. Take a little ride on my donkey. I love that donkey. Hell, I love everybody.

## W.S. Merwin

### Humble Beginning

When he had learned how to kill his brother with a rock he learned how to use a rock to begin stairs. For both of which secrets he thanked the rock.

He considered the rock further. It had always been there keeping secret what it could do. It had never so much as hinted at what it had already done. Now it was keeping all of its other secrets. He fell on his knees facing it and touched it with his forehead, his eyes, his nose, his lips, his tongue, his ears.

He thought the rock had created him. He thought that.

**Jamey Dunham**

## Urban Myth

A couple awaiting the arrival of their first-born delivers instead a ring-tailed lemur. They are beside themselves. The father beats the obstetrician with clenched fists. He curses the nurses and flings himself to the floor bawling. The mother stands up on the table and denounces God. The next day they go home. The lemur eats all of the houseplants and defecates in the sink. It refuses to come down from the refrigerator and keeps them up all night chasing flies along the window screens. The parents are mortified, but being optimistic people they remain patient. They dress the lemur as a boy and name it Colin. They send it to the finest schools and indulge it with every extravagance. Finally their hard work pays off. One morning upon entering the nursery they find a neat stack of money in the lemur's place.

## John Bradley

### Parable from Whence It all Began

Once, when there was only one word for people, and it was the same word as for the earth, I was human, with a body for a body, skin for skin, teeth for teeth, and hair. Hair everywhere. So much hair that after I left a place where I had slept, hair grew from the soil. But I was not afraid of Hair. I was afraid of the things Hair wanted me to do. Hair told me to climb to the top of a hollow tree and jump. Hair told me that I would fly—all the vibrating little hairs vibrating, carrying me on the wind. Hair told me to make love with my cousin the poplar. I knew this was wrong to make the trees have children. They would walk the land day and night on two legs saying, Am I a tree? Am I a human? Am I a human tree?

So I tore out my hair. I tore it out in handfuls. Threw it on the ground. Sprinkled salt on it. Hair growled. Hair wept. Hair promised never to flagellate with my hair. I stood there, looking at Hair dying in the grass. I knew Hair spoke lies. Hair would never change because Hair was Hair. I ran away. Hair found me again. But only some of Hair could tolerate me. The rest burned when it tried to root in me, leaving upon my skin scars the shape of open mouths. Now I am naked, nearly naked, Hair hiding in my armpit and groin and crotch. And they ask me, those last survivors of Hair, what I cannot ever know—Are you hair? Are you human? Are you human hair?

## Surreal Imagery/Narrative

When André Breton published his "Manifesto of Surrealism" in 1924, he not only formalized the Surrealist movement but contributed to its becoming one of the central influences not only on the prose poem but on culture in general in the twentieth century. Surrealists wanted to experience or to create the experience in an audience of what Breton called "the marvelous;" they sought to find it in "psychic automatism in its purest state," in collisions of the dream world and waking life. The effects in poetry were felt in verse and prose alike, but the prose poem was the perfect vessel for the dark, philosophical subtext of Surrealism. Some of the most celebrated contemporary prose poems can be seen to have a foot, if not a leg or two, in the school of Surrealist practice.

The poems represented here by Margarito Cuéllar, Eric Anderson, and Max Jacob all use surreal imagery effectively to convey the leap from observation to the subconscious. Cuéllar's poem follows the wandering mind of a speaker enraptured by the beauty of a secretary, while the speaker in Anderson's poem explores issues of love, dominance, and need with his dog. Jacob's poem "Hell Has Gradations" follows the descent of the speaker from the literal world to the figurative as he is pursued down a staircase to Hell. Russell Edson masterfully allows his poem "The Family Monkey" to frolic in both worlds interchangeably, and he somehow manages to steer the poem clear the trap of absurdity for its own sake. J. Marcus Weekley's "There is a White Man in My Soup" places mundane situations in a surreal narrative to comment subtly on class, race, and compassion. Finally we present here two selections from Charles Simic's *The World Doesn't End*, the first collection of prose poems to be awarded the Pulitzer Prize. The brief, semi-autobiographical prose poems employ dark, surreal images to capture the strange duality of an immigrant existing in two cultures, if not worlds, simultaneously.

## Margarito Cuéllar

### Ballad of the Carrot Girl

She could be a radish, a pore, a chambray onion. She grows in the summer, responding to the call of the sun. There's a double river in her eyes. Many would like to get tangled up in her waist like a happy shrub. Does she taste like raspberry gelatin? She crosses her legs and offers us (during office hours) a picture to mount. That glance of girlish thirst—surely she learned it in secretary school. She wants luck (there's no love to be found in us). And she drifts away, a capital letter, unpunctual, in her Monday afternoon flight.

*translated by Steven J. Stewart*

## Eric Anderson

### The Alpha Male

Every time the man puts on his shoes, his poor dog puts its tail down and says, So we're never going to see each other again.

There's no convincing the dog. Even when the man comes back from his errands, the dog rolls on the floor and cries, You're back! I thought I'd never see you again!

The man kneels and rubs the dog's ears with long, sympathetic strokes. He massages the soft tips, holds them between his fingers and thumbs.

And all that makes you the master and me the dog are those thumbs, the dog says. And a certain quantity of fur. And a tail, though I've seen the blunt knob where once you wagged around.

The man says, That was millions of years ago.

Think what I would do if I had thumbs. I could turn the knob on the door, hold the keys, learn to drive.

And then I might never see you again.

If only I had thumbs. Or then if you had no thumbs.

Now wait a minute, the man says. They both stare at his thumbs, plump as drumsticks on his hands. The man says, Let's not discuss the fur.

If only my feelings weren't told by this tail. Or then if my tail was yours.

My every emotion you'd know. I'd tuck my tail right now, roll at your feet.

Good dog, says the dog. Good dog!

## Max Jacob

### Hell Has Gradations

When I was working at the Fashion Cooperative I tried, despite the watchful eye of the dark, ugly old maid, to steal a pair of suspenders. I got chased down those splendid stairs not for the theft, but because I was a lazy worker who hated mindless finery. You descend, they follow. The stairs are less beautiful down by the offices than in the public area. They are less beautiful in shipping and handling than at the office level. They are even less beautiful down in the cellar! But what can I say about the swamp I came to? About the laughter? the animals I brushed against and the murmur of invisible things? The water turned into fire, my fear into a blackout. When I came to, I was in the hands of silent, unnamable surgeons.

*translated by William T. Kulik*

## Russell Edson

### The Family Monkey

We bought an electric monkey, experimenting rather recklessly with funds carefully gathered since grandfather's time for the purchase of a steam monkey.

We had either, by this time, the choice of an electric or gas monkey.

The steam monkey is no longer being made, said the monkey merchant.

But the family always planned on a steam monkey.

Well, said the monkey merchant, just as the wind-up monkey gave way to the steam monkey, the steam monkey has given way to the gas and electric monkeys.

Is that like the grandfather clock being replaced by the grandchild clock?

Sort of, said the monkey merchant.

So we bought the electric monkey, and plugged its umbilical cord into the wall.

The smoke coming out of its fur told us something was wrong.

We had electrocuted the family monkey.

## J. Marcus Weekley

### There is a White Man in My Soup

He yells a lot, like a boyfriend who wants all of my time, but at least he floats on a Y. Y is most like God, and this man asks too many questions, and his hair is too long, like a llama, but different. I ask him why he doesn't move to someone else's soup, like the lady in the leopard print dress, or the police officer with pink shoes. The white man asks me why I'm so much like a plane that's been shot down over the ocean, and I want to know who he thinks he is, why he's talking to me at all; I don't date men in my soup.

While the waitress asks me if I need anything else, the white man flirts with her, commenting on her perfume. She thanks him and I ask, "Can I have some more water, please," but she moves over to a guy in a gorilla suit. What has happened to the world? The white man asks me again why I'm so much like a plane that has been shot down over the ocean, and I start dunking him with my spoon. He's not drowning.

Embarrassed that someone will notice, I stop and look out the window at a lady who follows a golden chicken on a leash. She wears a wreath of fingers around her neck, and each of the fingernails is coated in emerald nail polish. The white man has moved to a B, and asks, "Why aren't you wearing any underwear?" Bs are so much like those annoying people at banks who don't wear deodorant and take six hours to process one transaction. Sick of this meal, I just want the white man to die, at least to get his ass out of my soup, so I can get back to work.

He latches on to my spoon, stands in the middle of it like a lizard on a rock, and I get ready to fling him into the cop's hair. "Wait. If you take me home, I'll love you forever. I'll even love you more than Snow White." And I cannot resist such an offer because I have lived my whole life like a poisonous apple or a piece of cloth which has been tucked into the pocket of a conductor waiting to blow his nose. The white man and I return to my office, where he is surprisingly quiet.

## Charles Simic

from *The World Doesn't End*

I was stolen by the gypsies. My parents stole me right back. Then the gypsies stole me again. This went on for some time. One minute I was in the caravan suckling the dark teat of my new mother, the next I sat at the long dining room tale eating my breakfast with a silver spoon.

It was the first day of spring. One of my fathers was singing in the bathtub; the other one was painting a live sparrow the colors of a tropical bird.

from *The World Doesn't End*

We were so poor I had to take the place of the bait in the mousetrap. All alone in the cellar, I could hear them pacing upstairs, tossing and turning in their beds. "These are dark and evil days," the mouse told me as he nibbled my ear. Years passed. My mother wore a cat-fur collar which she stroked until its sparks lit up the cellar.

# Rant

A rant can be defined loosely as an emotionally charged narrative or diatribe often expressing a strong distaste or anger on the one hand, or a declamatory, often pompous, assertion on the other. It is easy to see how the fluidity of the prose poem would lend itself to the rant. The prose poem's organization by sentence seems a natural fit for such rambling declarations as rants in speeches, formal letters and, of course, the op-ed section of the newspaper.

Jerry McGuire's "In Training" is a long, streaming trail of prose that shocks, delights, amuses, and captivates the reader with both its startling imagery and the sincere, frantic urgency of the narrative. Ginsberg's "A Supermarket in California" takes the reader along for a midnight stroll in the speaker's America where the rant is absorbed and ultimately resolved by the catalyst for the speakers sojourn: loneliness and the search for solidarity. Frank O'Hara's manic riff seems to want to equal all the energy of O'Hara's beloved Manhattan but is tempered with O'Hara's signature mix of humor, wit, and spontaneous bursts of beauty. Cornelius Eady, Peter Johnson, and Roxane Beth Johnson use the rant in the traditional sense, a straightforward vent that resonates long after the page, partially because of the language or an illuminating insight but primarily because of the brutal honesty the poem lays bare and the intense vulnerability of the speakers' last lines. Christopher Buckley and Radu Andriescu take aim at wider aspects of culture from dramatically different postures—Buckley's subtle, domestic, almost memoiristic personal narrative vs. Andriescu's energetic fragments that seem to want to get as much of the culture as possible into the poem.

## Jerry McGuire

In Training

I'm running down the street in my sister's prom gown yelling help me help me please won't someone help me and all around me are streamers and confetti with pretty strobes and background "Blue Bayou" on three Telecasters, bass, drums, and farfisa, but it's like someone flips a switch and then I'm ripping down the same street purple eye-shadow with starsparkles, yellowy rouge, crimson lips super shiny, lime-green hot pants and black mesh stiletto heels glue-on 2-inch nails with ecological blowjob pictures on them and screaming stop him! stop him! for fuck's sake won't somebody and there's this cacophony glitterball garland/minnelli/madonna jumble soundtrack with underneath it all the main theme from *Jaws* and then again and now my lungs are cracking, my feet drag heavy stones, cinder blocks, anvils wheeze and stagger step knees knock and wobble it's a polkadot housedress that shows my big tummy it rides up above the roll of my nylons I scream save me he's after me he's got my he took my he's going to please please I can't breathe, please and Perry Como's voice is going on in that sleepy thing so sexy and my toes are pinching my breasts bob and flop smack against my chin get stuck between my knees it's a duet Roscy Clooney *South Pacific* but I'm only fourteen my Catholic school plaids pumping field hockey fast down with DMX MF Doom and Nelly funky white girl Jockstrap Saves, Fuzzy Crackhole, Eat My Brain, Meat Mallets, Siamese Quadruplets, Sleater-Kinney, Be Good Tanyas, Sex Pastels, too cool for you, too cool for myself, crying mommy hurry he won't stop I'm alone I'm scared he just smiled I just smiled back I can't get away can't get away wicked pipes like Gypsies or Dervishes street full of broken glass my burka fights my body the elders want my clitoris I cry to them, to their goodness I cry to my mother I cry love I cry mercy

I cry to Allah I cry peace I cry and cry something I think the sound of men talking drowns me out nothing calls back to me, no quiet breath of incense and honey, no consolation the women turn their backs I'm honey-brown lambada legs scarlet dress the boys and girls all want to feel me can't keep their hands off I got this samba thing, merengue, sweet with light flashing first, next, last tango but running so dark, Cuban heels, music everywhere people all over the street they just look, like, hey, baby, can I have some of that, where you goin' in such a rush, it's all like *¡Basta, haz que se acabe! ¡No puedo soportarlo! ¡Por favor! No puedo respirar, ayudame, ayudame,* then all of a sudden it's more pretty, nice daylight I hear something behind me, people laughing, maybe, I'm running because everyone else is running I'm nine years old, it's 1972 big planes, the sky opens loud and orange my house goes funny colors barefoot on the road everyone barefoot running a hand or fierce hot wind comes and my clothes are gone I'm running my vagina so terror by an American shooting me with his camera no one can hear what I'm screaming, even me

**Peter Johnson**

## Overture

I'm sick of peekaboo metaphors, weary of mad stabs at uncertainty. And there's a guy making fun of my name, a nasty little prick with a Polaroid moment stuck in his head—his mother cheering as another perfect number two disappears down the drain. "Women get under things," Berryman said. Boy, did I like Berryman, though I'd been the first one to push him off a bridge. So go next store and order the Stud Muffin sandwich. Try to be friends with my son, talk about responsibility, watch his fingers tighten around a butter knife. And here's a joke laden with loot: We bought a little pug to forget about the TV. It ain't easy training a dog. It ain't easy living with all this cruelty. For example: How many people have I wished dead? None. How many injured? None. How many have made me sad? A great many. I count them while trying to fall asleep. And how's your Reuben? I ask. And how's your Stud Muffin? He asks back, then homeward where we take the pug for a walk, not talking, momentarily distracted by one of those ellipses which make certain historians want to slash their wrists. For them, just the facts, ma'am, always just the facts.

## Allen Ginsberg

### A Supermarket in California

What thoughts I have of you tonight, Walt Whitman, for I walked down the sidestreets under the trees with a headache self-conscious looking at the full moon.

In my hungry fatigue, and shopping for images, I went into a neon fruit supermarket, dreaming of your enumerations.

What peaches and what penumbras! Whole families shopping at night! Aisles full of husbands! Wives at the avocados, babies in the tomatoes!—and you, Garcia Lorca, what were you doing down by the watermelons?

I saw you, Walt Whitman, childless, lonely old grubber, poking among the meats in the refrigerator and eyeing the grocery boys.

I heard you asking questions of each: Who killed the pork chops? What price bananas? Are you my Angel?

I wandered in and out of the brilliant stacks of cans following you, and followed in my imagination by the store detective.

We strode down the open corridors together in our solitary fancy tasting artichokes, possessing every frozen delicacy, and never passing the cashier.

Where are we going, Walt Whitman? The doors close in an hour. Which way does your beard point tonight?

(I touch your book and dream of our odyssey in the supermarket and feel absurd.)

Will we walk all night through solitary streets? The trees add shade to shade, lights out in the houses, we'll both be lonely.

Will we stroll dreaming of the lost America of love past blue automobiles in driveways, home to our silent cottage?

Ah, dear father, graybeard, lonely old courage-teacher, what America did you have when Charon quit poling his ferry and you got out on a smoking bank and stood watching the boat disappear on the black waters of Lethe?

## Frank O'Hara

### Meditations in an Emergency

Am I to become profligate as if I were a blonde? Or religious as if I were French?

Each time my heart is broken it makes me feel more adventurous (and how the same names keep recurring on that interminable list!), but one of these days there'll be nothing left with which to venture forth.

Why should I share you? Why don't you get rid of someone else for a change?

I am the least difficult of men. All I want is boundless love.

Even trees understand me! Good heavens, I lie under them, too, don't I? I'm just like a pile of leaves.

However, I have never clogged myself with the praises of pastoral life, nor with nostalgia for an innocent past of perverted acts in pastures. No. One need never leave the confines of New York to get all the greenery one wishes—I can't even enjoy a blade of grass unless I know there's a subway handy, or a record store or some other sign that people do not totally regret life. It is more important to affirm the least sincere; the clouds get enough attention as it is and even they continue to pass. Do they know what they're missing? Uh huh.

My eyes are vague blue, like the sky, and change all the time; they are indiscriminate but fleeing, entirely specific and disloyal, so that no one trusts me. I am always looking away. Or again at something after it has given me up. It makes me restless and that makes me unhappy, but I cannot keep them still. If only I had grey, green, black, brown, yellow eyes; I would stay at home and do something. It's not that I'm curious. On the contrary, I am bored but it's my due to be attentive, I am needed by things as the sky must be above the earth. And lately, so great has their anxiety become, I can spare myself little sleep.

Now there is only one man I love to kiss when he is unshaven. Heterosexuality! You are inexorably approaching. (How discourage her?)

St. Serapion, I wrap myself in the robes of your whiteness which is like midnight in Dostoevsky. How am I to become a legend, my dear? I've tried love, but that hides you in the bosom of another and I am always springing forth from it like the lotus—the ecstasy of a hyacinth, "to keep the filth of life away," yes, there, even in the heart, where the filth is pumped in and slanders and pollutes and determines. I will my will, though I may become famous for a mysterious vacancy in that department, that greenhouse.

Destroy yourself, if you don't know!

It is easy to be beautiful; it is difficult to appear so. I admire you, beloved, for the trap you've set. It's like a final chapter no one reads because the plot is over.

"Fanny Brown is run away—scampered off with a Cornet of Horses; I do love that little Minx, & hope She may be happy, tho' She has vexed by this Exploit a little too. –Poor silly Cecchina! Or F:B: as used to call her. –I wish She had a good Whipping and 10,000 pounds."—Mrs. Thrale.

I've got to get out of here. I choose a piece of shawl and my dirtiest suntans. I'll be back, I'll re-emerge, defeated, from the valley; you don't want me to go where you go, so I go where you don't want me to. It's only afternoon, there's a lot ahead. There won't be any mail downstairs. Turning, I spit in the lock and the knob turns.

## Cornelius Eady

### Motherless Children

How many ways do I want to kill this woman, this young bureaucrat at the Office of Social Services, for wanting to kill me? Kill me slowly by degrees, kill me with provisions, kill me in measured words, kill my mother by rubbing her sad life with my father in her face. O, how this woman, bored, dulled by repetition, wants my mother officially rendered inert, reduced to a mere boarder in a broken-down ghetto house, how she wants the word bastard to define our conversation.

What did I say or do? Who knows, but I do know this look she's giving me, after telling me that there's no place for my mother's well-being in their guidelines, that as far as they're concerned, she isn't even legally a part of my family. I know this look. This woman wants to observe a screamer, a ripper, she wants her dreams of a babbling monkey to rise.

Blow up, she whispers, as she explains what she isn't going to do for me, how my father's bound to disappear, item by item, first his house, then his cars, then all his money except for what it takes for a pine box and a hole.

She thinks she's the facts of life, a wall with no apparent handholds, the river referred to in the old spirituals: deep, wide, fraught with many sorrows, and her eyes dare me to become a nigger and kick over the table.

**Roxane Beth Johnson**

## Middle Passage

Don't give me no words on a page to describe my sufferings. Don't tell me you can speak the stench rising up thick as flies. I'll tell you my eyes burned with piss and the sun lit on nothing but the bleeding wounds on my back. Don't worry about me now, packed tight in that slop jar holding the slippery hip of some woman ain't mine. I got no lessons from the dying, no peace from the spirits I begged to help us. I tell you none of them came, though I always gave them meat. Don't look at me with your pity. I don't cry no tears. Ever. The taste just reminds me of the sea.

## Christopher Buckley

### Conspiracy Theory: Low Carb Diet Conversion

Sweet Jesus, there's no way. I'm living it up with a Ry Krisp Light, an edge of Parmesan, a 6 oz glass of wine. It's the crackers levitating my cells and shouting Hallelujah. These days, it's all fishes, no loaves—not now, not ever again. These holey biscuits (and only a few) are all that are given unto me.

I've dropped 40 lbs. with another boat-load to go. Another platter of lettuce with vinegar on the side. I can eat eggs and all the animals I can get my hands on, my cholesterol shooting up like Southern California real estate prices. What I wouldn't give to be as emaciated as a saint, born-lucky, thin-boned, biologically redeemed from the get-go.

I'm trying to keep the gears and gizmos in the ticker ticking without electrical hiccups, without the ventricle bulking up like Schwarzenegger's biceps in his robot movies, and one day locking up in what my cardiologist mechanically refers to as the light bulb blowing out.

"This Is Your Life," as Ralph Edwards said in the '50s on TV—it's black and white. He's long gone to his reward, but if he's lucky, they're not eating skinless chicken breasts and broccoli 7 nights a week in the afterlife. In any case, I'm not ready to look back from wherever it is you get good reception.

For all I know, the soul in its grey shirttails and gamma rays circles the sky over a car-wash in Beirut, making amends for the shortcomings of the past. Hell, it might hover anywhere in the Middle East where there are no bombs or land mines, where even the poor—which is most everybody—sit down to stuffed grape leaves, hummus, baba ganoush, and celestial loaves of pita bread, steam rising like prayer without anyone giving the first thought to arteriosclerosis. If I found a family well enough off I could partake of a lamb's grilled leg, some cucumber sauce, a glass of cloud juice, and a bitter herb or two, but that's the limit.

In Iraq, armored personnel carriers and GIs sweep through the streets, handing out MREs and Hershey bars to kids as if WW II never ended, as if Vietnam's weekly TV slot had not been finally cancelled—bodies still stacking up like leaking sacks of rice. It's the same ballgame, they just keep changing the pitchers. And given the pastime of organized national aggression, everyone's blood pressure is climbing like gasoline prices, and not just from the usual stress at the job, or the salt on the fries with that Whopper I'm not having for lunch.

Half the poor souls in the desert would praise the Lord for a box of Ry Krisp. But I'm bitter and disillusioned reading the labels—99 out of 100 companies adding sugar to everything—peas, carrots, tomatoes, even asparagus for Christ's sake—or not—and charging more. I should have bought stock in the omniscient high fructose corn syrup conglomerates, the ones with Dick Cheney on their Board of Directors. Sugar in breads, in fruit juice, in cereal, protein bars, processed lunch meats—you name it—none of which, for all my sins, I'm ever going to enjoy again. My bowl is filled with hard green pepper, celery, miserable arugula, soggy soy sprouts, and a slice of unmarinated muscle. And though it's written in the wisdom of the fathers that all things are possible, there seems precious little of that on the menu these days. Look around and it's easy to see that someone's always getting fat killing off the rest of us.

## Radu Andriescu

### the aswan high dam

*fuck sex*, written across the chest of a kid in the internet café... a pasty face, chrysanthemum pimples... computer cases for everyone: for andradu... i can't read fortunes in azure coffee... the sky shines clear on the outside... but inside, empty... like classrooms these last three days... the rest, inevitably, will come to be... *graduation*, *gradualism*... stadium tiers of seats for an everyday circus... the sun is blazing, at the moment... and it's cool... radu drank a huge coffee at the economics faculty... a laborer on the rich soil of culture... i want so much to write a socialistrealist poem, but one which wouldn't have to be *ironically recovered*... the paleolithic mask of the workingman... the imperial crown of the bronze-age man... big bill broonzy... packs of young pioneers in copou park... a pioneer's red scarf... mark rothko or ellsworth kelly... *orange and yellow* or *the wright curve*... unicef designs... colored chalk on the park walkways... unicef cards, fall after fall... money for burkina faso... ouagadougou... the pheromonal honey of wild bees... raking leaves... greenhouses hidden in the recesses of copou... a classmate demonstrating how he can eat earthworms and beetles... it must have been sixth grade when he grew a beard and moustache... a hirsute man among beardless youths... in eighth grade he stopped growing... he turned into a short little man who very quickly went bald...

biographemes, glyphs of memory... podu iloaiei, a small town near iaşi ... the center of nothingness... the horsefly girl with green-eyed thought... the windowless minivan... the writers from iaşi, country roads... anachronism, anacondism... the circle... literary circles, never concentric... the wheels of the pioneer bicycle... dull red... but first, the blue scooter, copou park, the paternal glyph, the lamppost-with-a-glass-lantern-in-the-form-of-a-truncated-cone glyph... the drinking fountain glyph, the mosquito swarm glyph, the evening glyph, the overjoyed glyph... the pegasus bike... the mother-of-pearl red bike... two luminous wings, the horns of siameze unicorns... the glyph camelia, the blonde who lived next door... the monaxial-verticalswing glyph... the chestnut tree glyph, the hollow in the tree glyph... the cigarette pack glyph, the illicit glyph, the braces-on-my-teeth glyph, the monaxial-horizontal-swing glyph... the hugefisheye-with-ceramic-eyelids glyph, the snail-egg-the-size-of-a-crystal-globe glyph... the indecipherable glyph of friendship...

ouahigouya, koudougou, tenkodogo, niangoloko, aribinda, faramana, koupéla... the grundig portable recorder... barry white... the glyph anca, the bîrnova forest glyph, the brobdingnagian burdock-leaf glyph, the incandescent glyph, the train station glyph… madjori, bodo-dioulasso, banfora, kourou, gaoua, kaya... dori, léo, sanga, pô... the republic of mongoosia, the yellow-green flag, the vinyl constitution, the boomerang of a maple seed, the coup d'état of the chestnut, white mulberry mead... the carpathian bicycle, simple, black, solid… the sputnik bicycle, blue, with a broken gear… the peugeot bicycle, up in tudor's attic... master ursachi's poetical bicycle... the bike that must never be sold... the magisterial glyph... the square stone of night, the center of chaos, the telemobile crystal... radu's exit... the definitive departure from radu... of the spacc carved in stone... *rubble*... hydrogen peroxide on the lacerated knee... the sting-on-raw-flesh glyph... the painful froth... the house at the end of the woods... the gallic car... socialist realism and muscovite conceptualism... socialist realism and calcium carbide... socialist realism and amiri baraka... from motherboard to motherboard through the viscera of the server...

glyphs zero and one… phonograms, ideograms… photograms, factograms, fracturograms, miserygrams… the black volta, the red volta, the white volta… the merciful god of the wild honeybee… the glyph marx/catargi street… the glyphs shot into the walls of the regional radio studios… the glyph county secretary… the glyph warm at work cold at home… the glyph carved into the tip of a finger, the glyph carved on the martian belly… it's just a matter of perspective… the glyph dickinson, the glyph whitman… the glyph badge of honor, the glyph glass cabinet, the glyph chinese fisherman… the glyph in the seraglio…the native glyph, the allogeneic glyph… ciric lake… breaking up on the bridge… breaking up on the island… from *concept* to *discept*…

*the electrical snow*… tetecoşovei... *la guerra elletrica*... marinetti... an accident in the twisting / of many and diverse "thoughts" / i.e. nerves, glandular facilities, *electrical cranial charges*... zukofsky... since the upper paleolithic, wick has become fuse as the conveyor of ignition for *electrical purposes as well as for shells and bombs.* "juniper fuse," then, as a metaphor connecting the flame by which cave imagery was made possible to its ignescent consequences in modern life... eshelman... when the hard drive on the pc that controls the security system crashes, every fire door in the hotel—each held open by *electrically controlled magnets*—slams shut. cardinals will take some getting used to... silliman...

There is certainly plenty of monotony in the 150-page title poem... but it is the fertile kind, which generates excitement as water monotonously flowing over a dam generates electrical power.... ashbery / stein... then the day came: the egyptian government sent me on a generous mission fellowship to study in america for a ph.d. in *electrical engineering* and return to help build the aswan high dam... ihab hassan...

it comes through the brain's static, / *electrical stutter at synapse*, / through the moiré of light crossing light... wendy battin... stout as a horse, affectionate, haughty, *electrical*, / i and this mystery here we stand... i sing the *body electric*... whitman...

Powerful Herbal Products Help Cleanse and Nourish Your Electrical Body

P.S. ...also i'm interested in such analogies with modern poetry as that provided by the vacuum tube. the latter can tap a huge reservoir of *electrical energy*, picking it up as a very weak impulse. then it can shape it and amplify it to major intensity. technique of allusion as you use it (situational analogies) seems comparable to this type of circuit. allusion not as ornament but as precise means of making available total energy of any previous situation or culture. shaping and amplifying it for current use... mcluhan / pound...

*translated by Adam J. Sorkin and the poet*

## Essayistic

The essayistic prose poem employs conventions typically associated with nonfiction essays more than with poetry—it may use flat language, tends to focus more on content than on style, begins with a fact or an object as its starting point—in order to arrive at comparisons, equivalences, or arguments that inhere in the content of the poem.

Two of the pieces in this section, R. L. Rimas's "House by the Railroad" and Jeff Davis's "Source," take paintings as their leaping off points, using both anecdote and textual reference in implied arguments about American-ness in art (Rimas) and the roles of abstraction and image on natural, personal, and political levels (Davis). Christopher Buckley uses elements of memoir (personal history, anecdote, reflection) in a mini-essay that begins with musings on the poet's age but eventually leads us to musings about the age of the universe. Fanny Howe's "Doubt," one of the most acclaimed prose poems in recent years, uses facts from the lives of several writers as touchstones for a tour de force meditation on the title, its flip-side, and their fluctuations along the nodes of time and history—much like the way a thoughtful essayist might try on different sides of an argument rather than simply pick a side and argue it with blinders on. Jeff Harrison's "4th Missive" combines scientific, quasi-scientific, and pseudo-scientific elements in a wrapper of common argumentative rhetoric, parodying the idea of the essay as an objective rhetorical form.

Recently the term "lyric essay" has come into fashion, and many of the poems in this book, in addition to the "essayistic prose poems" offered here, might fit into that classification.

**R. L. Rimas**

## House by the Railroad

*after an Edward Hopper painting*

1.
Hopper writes in *The Arts*, "Charles Burchfield: American:"

And why need we copy the Doric or the Gothic model? Beauty, convenience, grandeur of thought and quaint expression are as near to us as to any, and if the American artist will study with hope and love for the precise thing to be done by him, considering the climate, the soil, the length of the day, the wants of the people, the habit and form of the government, he will create a house in which all these will find themselves fitted, and taste and sentiment will be satisfied also.

2.
Imitating French impressionists, Hopper received little commercial success at exhibitions for his paintings. It took Hopper the better half of 20 years to find the style that made his paintings American, though secretly he preferred the title Impressionist.

3.
He later cultivated a practice that Degas supposedly affected, a practice of incomplete disclosure. His was a personality half-illuminated by fact, & the other conjured in the imagination of his critics.

4.
Edward Hopper was an American Giorgio de Chirico or an up to date Vermeer, yet painting in the contemporary vernacular of his time. This perhaps should interest us only as a sidenote.

5.
Born in Nyack, New York, a town on the Hudson River. Descended from an old Dutch family, Hopper was reared on the conservative Victorian values.

He grew up in a world come undone: the horse-drawn carriage soon gave way to the automobile; women, as the popular consensus of the time prohibited, were not good drivers—biologically speaking...

6.
His mother was quite a force, I'm told. Proud. Doting. A tyrant of the household who had better business sense than his ineffectual father, who was, as Hopper recalls, a closet intellectual.

7.
Hopper often quotes Emerson at length in the articles he wrote for *The Arts*. He liked Sherwood Anderson well enough, even Hemingway too, but thought little of other Modernists, preferring their Atlantic predecessors, French symbolists & the like.

8.
The house in which we find ourselves is the one built by Hopper's own contrarian nature, at odds with his fascination & his distaste for the innovation of the 20th century (he loved the cinema, but he was shocked by contraceptives).

9.
This is distilled within “House by the Railroad,” a work finished in 1925, which is early in the spectrum of his greater works, but late in his life. He had the lean look of an artist by 29, & looked twice as haggard by the time his career took off like a run-away automobile. With more than a dozen exhibitions under his belt, he failed in his first years to obtain the success that Robert Henri or George Bellows received.

10.
“House by the Railroad” possesses no likely doors, forever denying certitude in the face of inquiry by its viewers, a house possessed of itself. Like a self-contained labyrinth, as in de Chirico’s “Mystery and Melancholy of a Street,” the painting dares us to question, though the shutters are drawn & the darkness within stifles all vision. Our answers are never complete. In the waning afternoon light the house appears to us as a monolith in very much the same way the Pyramids of Giza entertain our curiosity.

11.
Undeniably American, “House by the Railroad” was inspired by a house Hopper had seen in France in 1909 and loved. The Mansard roof is one of Hopper’s motifs, encoded like a cryptic communiqué between spies.

## Jeff Davis

### The Source

It should suffice to say that Rothko's early painting "The Source" contains two forms: one form is oblong, a floating pendant from Costa Rica or a flat mask from Zaire, scar lines down its nose; the other, a shrunken, elongated Giacometti, a charm piece or bone flute from Peru, textured by some cheap painter's trick.

Maybe one form becomes a flattened gray tick, blood speckled, and the other a painted clothespin or fishing lure: the more domestic, familiar comparisons become bastard boys who try not only to break their way into quiet homes but—like Valery's Rimbaud—to replace their impotent fathers.

But comparisons deceive. Rothko desired no facsimiles of more real patterns, wanted not to play the carnival wizard pulling switches and levers to thrill adolescent audiences in love with themselves, with cheap thrills that recreate nature and ecstasy in the mind. 100 years or so before Rothko, Louis Daguerre's wife called him a lunatic for fixing images in photographs. So I imagine Rothko, frustrated with nature, closes his eyes more tightly than Cezanne to see and to slam the door on the boys who try to enter.

His estate holds no sketches that resemble DaVinci's renditions of defined torsos with measured bodies or Vesalius's illustrations of femurs and intestines that appear the year Copernicus completes Revolutions of Celestial Orbs. In the 1950's, while Rothko develops a "mature style" of pure abstraction, scientists amplify light by stimulated emissions of radiation. Image becomes a verb, to image, imaging, says some kid chemist, he among the first generation of scientists whose imaginations have been imprinted by televised projections of Donna Reed or Jackie Gleason, now among the clan concocting color maps of brain impulses, of liver interiors, of June bug wings, of bacteria graphed and colored like tiny roller paint brushes along pin heads and scotch tape strips, the structure of a thunderstorm codified into computer dots & lines, a mockingbird's song tacked by color & line according to frequency, pitch, amplitude, tonal pattern, charted and given numbers called "raw data" (a sound ascribed a number like a chemical, e.g., gold becomes Au 79).

Rothko sensed the danger of trying to render nature, to divide it and apportion it into a frame as if our senses and ability to calculate alone could comprehend it. In Boulder last summer I saw retailers selling Lakota tobacco ties for $6. A Ghost Dance dress: $3,800. A totem pole: $850.

So where, or how, does an artist go? Manet goes to color patches to distort the eye, while a Hopi woman, face captured in a film documentary, speaks of how she receives patterns of lines in dreams and cannot rest easy until she transforms those patterns in clay, zig-zag, zig-zag, one line responding and referring only to other lines, pure lineage within the bowl's walls curved to act as receptacles of ornament, function, symbol in one.

## Christopher Buckley

### Eternity (being a condensed spiritual and aesthetic biography)

*for VS*

No one says I look 55—no one says I don't, except my new friend Virgil. He has two catholic daughters and like me, hates to fly, but there's not other way to get home in time for the youngest's 1st Communion. I almost remember mine… I've been scared ever since—of Death, of course. You tell me why… In 2nd grade, the nun lectured us about Eternity, which almost arrived later from Cuba in the early '60s, Cuba where my friend Virgil was born, which has at least one entrance to hell and exits in Spain and L.A. In the afterlife, I don't think anyone is rolling cigars while someone reads them Don Quixote in the original. Anyway, we were going to spend Eternity in hell if we did not do as we were told. Sister explained that Eternity was like an enormous steel ball, the size of the earth, upon which an eagle, gliding in from the cosmic starry dark beyond Cleveland and the east coast, once every million years, landed and took off again. The time it took that steel ball to completely wear away from the friction of the eagle landing and lifting away was less than a second of Eternity, the time we'd be burning on a hot rock for cussing, eating hot dogs on Friday, not making our yearly Easter obligation of communion or mass, or having impure thoughts about Belinda Sanchez. Go figure.

What if, on the practical side, the universe—and so time-space—does curve back on itself like a huge quesadilla? We're going nowhere. What, then, have we been suffering for all along? More specifically, what have I been doing here with that image like a fish hook in my brain for 48 years? Nuns, with their psycho-spiritual hammer-locks, were terrorists, and they did not discriminate among ages or ethnic groups. Death, darkness, and sure damnation were there equally for us all if we didn't stop talking during mass and go out and finagle quarters from relatives and folks on our block for the pagan babies. Dear God.

I don't know what angel brings me these lines in the middle of the night after I'm up and down the hall to the bathroom, brings them every few years like a palm tree and a pool of water appearing after sands have shifted for no reason, like some metaphysical crust of light. Some angel sweeping down with dust, one in the back of the chorus singing hosannas like nobody's business who has a little time to spare, and angel who every now and then hands off a few imagistic granules while I'm flaming away here in the flesh, in darkness where I wouldn't know the source but would know a gift when I heard one.

Once I'm half awake and the cells are ticking over like new stars, I lose track of time and switch the lamp on and off and write down phrases, losing sleep—what does it come to? The door of a '59 Chevy swings open like a vault and lets out some earlier, more sprightly version of me, only a few blocks from happiness, or the sea, whichever comes first—with my papers and a new poem in hand—more than I arrived with. Who knew where I was headed? The nuns were sure: Hell. Virgil and I voted for Spain, even southern California if that's the best we could do to breathe cool salt air. Maybe I could do this forever, who knows? As I was taught, worse things could happen to me. Outside of Time, will poems matter? Why ask now—I'm not an academic, an administrator, slick in a Republican suit. We're not for long, not forever. Death, of course. And next? I hope it's not hell, or anywhere near Pennsylvania, where I already served a ten year Purgatory.

Dear God. Thank you for the gift of the eccentric brain, this associative jelly. Thank you for this moonraking poem which keeps me alive in prayer, in doubt, and in hope. This poem which for once did not take 5 months and 50 drafts, though I would have waited patiently as always—like salt dissolving from the sea, like air gathering to be somewhere else, like the last flake of rust outside of time....

## Fanny Howe

### Doubt

Virginia Woolf committed suicide in 1941 when the German bombing campaign against England was at its peak and when she was reading Freud whom she had staved off until then.

Edith Stein, recently and controversially beatified by the Pope, who had successfully worked to transform an existential vocabulary into a theological one, was taken to Auschwitz in August, 1942.

One year later Simone Weil died in a hospital in England—of illness and depression—determined to know what it is to know. She, as much as Woolf, sought salvation in a choice of words.

But multitudes succumb to the sorrow induced by an inexact vocabulary.

While a whole change in discourse is a sign of conversion, the alteration of single word only signals a kind of doubt about the value of the surrounding words.

Poets tend to hover over words in this troubled state of mind. What holds them poised in this position is the occasional eruption of happiness.

While we would all like to know if the individual person is a phenomenon either culturally or spiritually conceived and why everyone doesn't kill everyone else, including themselves, since they can—poets act out the problem with their words.

Why not say "heart-sick" instead of "despairing"?
Why not say "despairing" instead of "depressed"?

Is there, perhaps, a quality in each person—hidden like a laugh inside a sob—that loves even more than it loves to live? If there is, can it be expressed in the form of the lyric line?

Dostoevsky defended his later religious belief, saying of his work, "Even in Europe there have never been atheistic expressions of such power. My hosannah has gone through a great furnace of doubt."

According to certain friends, Simone Weil would have given everything she wrote to be a poet. It was an ideal but she was wary of charm and the inauthentic. She saw herself as stuck in fact with a rational prose line for her surgery on modern thought. She might be the archetypal doubter but the language of the lyric was perhaps too uncertain.

Yet Weil could be called a poet, if Wittgenstein could, despite her own estimation of her writing, because of the longing for a transformative insight dominating her word choices.

In "Prelude" the narrator is an uprooted seeker who still hopes that a conversion will come to her from the outside. The desired teacher arrives bearing the best of everything, including delicious wine and bread, affection, tolerance, solidarity (people come and go) and authority. This is a man who even has faith and loves truth.

She is happy. Then suddenly, without any cause, he tells her it's over. She is out on the streets without direction, without memory. Indeed she is unable to remember even what he told her without his presence there to repeat it, this is amnesia being the ultimate dereliction.

If memory fails, then the mind is air in a skull. This loss of memory forces her to abandon hope for either rescue or certainty.

And now is the moment where doubt—as an active function—emerges and magnifies the world. It eliminates memory. And it turns eyesight so far outwards, the vision expands. A person feels as if she is the figure inside a mirror, looking outwards for her moves. She is a forgery.

When all the structures granted by common agreement fall away and that "reliable chain of cause and effect" that Hannah Arendt talks about—breaks—then a person's inner logic also collapses. She moves and sees at the same time, which is terrifying.

Yet strangely it is in this moment that doubt shows itself to be the physical double to belief; it is the quality that nourishes willpower, and the one that is the invisible engine behind every step taken. Doubt is what allows a single gesture to have a heart.

In this prose poem Weil's narrator recovers her balance after a series of reactive revulsions to the surrounding culture by confessing to the most palpable human wish: that whoever he was, he loved her.

Hope seems to resist extermination as much as a roach does.

Hannah Arendt talks about the "abyss of nothingness that opens up before any deed that cannot be accounted for." Consciousness of this abyss is the source of belief for most converts. Weil's conviction that evil proves the existence of God is cut out of the consciousness.

Her Terrible Prayer—that she be reduced to a paralyzed nobody—desires an obedience to that moment where coming and going intersect before annihilation.

And her desire: "To be only an intermediary between the blank page and the poem" is a desire for a whole-heartedness that eliminates personality.

Virginia Woolf, a maestro of lyric resistance, was frightened by Freud's claustrophobic determinism since she had no ground of defense against it. The hideous vocabulary of mental science crushed her dazzling star-thoughts into powder and brought her latent despair into the open air. Born into a family devoted to skepticism and experiment, she had made a superhuman effort at creating a prose-world where doubt was a mesmerizing and glorious force.

Anyone who tries, as she did, out of a systematic training in secularism, to forge a rhetoric of belief is fighting against the odds. Disappointments are everywhere waiting to catch you, and an ironic realism is so convincing.

Simone Weil's family was skeptical too, secular and attentive to the development of the mind. Her older brother fed her early sense of inferiority with his condescending intellectual putdowns. Later, her notebooks chart a superhuman effort at conversion to a belief in affliction as a sign of God's presence.

Her prose itself is tense with effort. After all, to convert by choice (that is, without a blast of revelation or a personal disaster) requires that you shift the names for things, and force a new language out of your mind onto the page.

You have to make yourself believe. Is this possible? Can you turn "void" into "God" by switching the words over and over again? Any act of self-salvation is a problem because of death which always has the last laugh, and if there has been a dramatic and continual despair hanging over childhood, then it may even be impossible.

After all, can you call "doubt" "bewilderment" and suddenly be relieved?

Not if your mind has been fatally poisoned... But even then, it seems, the dream of having no doubt continues, finding its way into love and work where choices matter exactly as much as they don't matter—when history's things are working in your favor.

**Jeff Harrison**

High up in the Froth of the Accursed (4th Missive)

Me? I like best the super-wolves that were seen to cross the sun during the earthquake at Palermo. They howled. Or the loves of the worlds. The howls of the planets. I suppose deep-sea fishes have their noses bumped by cinders. All sciences begin with the attempt to define. Nothing has ever been defined. There is nothing to define. Darwin wrote *The Origin Of The Species*. He was never able to define what he meant by "species." It is not possible to define. Nothing has ever been finally found out. There is nothing to find out—it's like looking for a needle that no one ever lost in a haystack that never was stacked. But all scientific attempts really to find out something, whereas really there is nothing to find out, are attempts, themselves, really to be something. We are not realists nor idealists we are intermediatists.

I think that one is likely to smile incredulously at the notion of blue moons. NEVERTHELESS they were as common in 1883 as were green suns in 1883. The Earth complained to Mars & swore a vast oath at us. Little frogs start hopping—knowing no more what it's about than we do when we crawl to work in the morning and hop away at night.

Bacteria could survive in what we call outer space, of which we know nothing. If you'd like to have a chemist's opinion, even though it is only a chemist's opinion, see the report of the meeting of the Royal Chemical Society, April 2, 1903. If there were elements there could be a real science of chemistry. A coin is condemned because it came from the same region from which, a few years before, had come pottery that had become fraudulent. Hair called real hair—then there are wigs. Teeth called real teeth—then there are dentures. Official money—counterfeit money. Some third-rate scientist comes out with an explanation of the vermiform appendix that would have been acceptable to the biblical Moses. The twinkling of stars is the penetration of light through something that quivers.

IT WOULD BE ABSURD TO SAY THE WHOLE SKY IS GELATINOUS: it seems more acceptable to say only certain areas are gelatinous. It is safe to say most of us are deep-sea fishes of a kind—iron, nickel, butter, paper, wool, silk resin, beef, blood, and stone are these kinds of deep-sea fishes. Lucifer never fell from the Heavens—there was Adam in the first place & a human being attracts lightning—the lightning was seen and mistaken for a falling angel when it was just Adam in the first place & a close call it was with the lightning. Science relates to real knowledge no more than the growth of a plant or the organization of a department store or the development of a nation. I know of no difference between science and Christian Science, a Lord Kelvin and a Mrs. Eddy. A Christian Scientist and a toothache—neither exists in the final sense.

In 1859 the thing to do was to accept Darwinism but Darwinism was never proved: the fittest survive. What is meant by the fittest? Not the strongest, not the cleverest—weakness and stupidity everywhere survive. There is no way of determining fitness except in that a thing does survive. "Fitness," then, is only another name for "survival." Darwinism: that survivors survive. Survival of the survivors. A cultural revolution ignited by a tautology. The little harlots will caper and freaks will distract attention and clowns will break the rhythm of the whole with their buffooneries—but the solidity of the procession as a whole and the impressiveness of things that pass and pass and pass will keep on and keep on and keep on coming.

Venus de Milo—to a child she is repellent. Never has a chemical law, without exception, been discovered—chemistry is continuous with astronomy physics biology. For instance, if the sun should greatly change its distance from the Earth the familiar chemic formulas would no longer work out. There is only in human experience intermediateness to harmony and discord. Harmony is that besides which there are no outside forces. All biologic phenomena act to adjust—there are no biologic actions other than adjustment. As distinct from vegetables, animals do not exist. Newton's three laws, or three attempts to break continuity, are as unreal as all other attempts to localize the universal. Newton's three laws are three articles of faith. Demons and angels and inertias and reactions are all mythological characters.

If there are cats, they're only an emphasis upon universal felinity. If everything else is variable, the notion of gravitation as fixed and formulable is only another attempted positivism. Though gravitation may approximate higher to invariability than do the winds, it must be somewhere between the absolutes of stability and instability. The language of physicists and astronomers is the language of expiring sibilations. Astronomers are mercantile purists who would deny commercial vagabondage. Astronomy is a phantom-film distended with myth-stuff. In a real existence, such a quasi-system of fables as the science of chemistry could not deceive for a moment—but that in an existence attempting to become real, it represents that attempt.

## Poems of Address/Epistolary Poems

Among poems of address, the epistolary poem is the most commonly used and the best known; but prose poets tend to look for wide varieties of cultural discourse as models for their poems and have found use in forms of address such as the public address announcement (see the William Matthews poem in this section) and the valediction (see Steve Wilson's poem here).

This section includes several different varieties of epistolary poems, based on different types of letters—intimate letters, cover letters, political letters. The epistolary poem, when done successfully, uses the relationship between addressor and the addressee to engage the reader. The poem appears to be a genuine correspondence or, at the very least, allows the readers to follow along in a state of suspended disbelief. The poem can convey a sense of urgency and even trust to the reader, allowing an almost voyeuristic glimpse into the world the poem encapsulates.

The epistolary poems of Geraldine Monk and Susan Briante take bold liberties with the reader's expectations for the form. Their use of vivid imagery and an ironic, often exaggerated narrative constantly surprises. Monk's poem is from a sequence based on actual letters between Mary, Queen of Scots and Elizabeth I. The poem "Letter to Carlos Pellicer" by Eunice Odio takes a more direct approach as it references the late poet Carlos Pellicer and, in particular, his collection *Hora de Junio*—it is a poem that is an actual letter, as opposed to a poem simply using the conventions of letters. Like the two poems before it, Odio's poem is rich in imagery and abstract in the progression of its narrative; but here the technique is used to a different end. Amy Newman's poem is from a sequence of poems that take the form of cover letters to editors as a way of transgressing the nature of the relationship between author and editor.

## Geraldine Monk

To the High and Mighty Etcetera,

I salute your intelligence even though that very word doubles its bluff with false wars and sexes-up a damp squib to apocalyptic tyrannical paranoia—I get carried away before I am carried away but before I am carried I must acquaint you with my state as briefly as can be: my batteries are going flat. The feathers from my Byrds of America are losing colour with my absence. This is no light matter.

Apropos of nothing. Is this the "beautiful game" my voices speak? Two queens squaring upnoses cross nor/sou divide beneath t'transit of Venus? The sun sunders under-clout never putting fangs or milk pegs forth in this godforsook sunlessland to cut a dash and toast the heart full score. This sentence is too long. I apologise. But mine is too—too long. If this is a game—is it in two halves? And who's the referee? You may have heard I'm going deaf from lack of laughter.

My days weigh with interminable seconds. I pick up knowledge beyond my years. An inferno breaks my sleep. A centre of industry will spring around my feet. Steel light the fandango night sky will flare and vanish in decades. With nothing in my present to engage I read the past and future terribly. I cry nightly for the Buffer Girls. Diamonds in brown paper. Ada. Oh. Lived-in lovely Ada.

I have taken up arms against my me. By unexpected means I try to die driven by the devil knows who. Almighty Disposer of all things please deliver me. I have lost a battle and loyal pals fell before my eyes I have no hope but your goodness for without that

I cannot imagine the back of beyond nor see the broad streets of my afterlife. I miss my feathers

dearly,
Your affectionate sister

Millithrum Queet Spick.

## Susan Briante

### DEAR MR. CHAIRMAN OF ETHICS, LEADERSHIP AND PERSONNEL POLICY IN THE US ARMY'S OFFICE OF THE DEPUTY CHIEF OF STAFF FOR PERSONNEL

First, let me explain: My mother forbade me to walk fence rails with the Maleski boy. She barred me from taking off my shirt to dig flowerbeds with the Holloway girl. I kicked an overturned coffee can in the middle of the cul-de-sac. Storm after storm blew past the screen door. Standing under the plum tree's pale pink blossoms was putting on a veil.

In the hard soil of childhood, God was everywhere: in pitted sycamores, a vibrating clothes line, in fireflies hung still as lanterns from a Japanese maple.

One day I carved a whole landscape in the windowsill. Sun, willow, car, lady. Perhaps there were rabbits. My mother grabbed my wrist: a transformer exploded, the rains broke, live wires writhed like eels through our streets.

How much loneliness must we inherit?

So, Sir, I grew earth-bound and cursed: a quarry, a cavernous construction site. God lagged behind in the pale light of swimming pools and pines. I took lovers and planes. In the desert east of Palm Springs, I drove past windmills flapping like dancers, like angels trying to redirect traffic.

Yes, that was me, kneeling down to take a birth control pill by baggage claim area three.

Of course, Sir, I can see it clearly now. Where once there was a thicket, I recognize three trees. A complicated song: a cardinal's call, a mother's, voice, a wedding march. I want to undo it. Wind brings one bush to thrash and panic while another remains still as porcelain. Promiscuity, like a season, has its limit. Inevitably, rain weaves a sort of loose net on the window screen. Any woman of a certain age will recognize it as cheap lace.

## Eunice Odio

### Letter to Carlos Pellicer

Most precious sir, most sapient child:

Today, which is The June Hour, I'm going to present you a few things that belong to me: a drop of Sun; a blue that I found on the street, the second half of a swallow; the mantle of an insect the color of earth; some diamond-like, multitudinous dreams. Do you like these celestial objects? Do you accept them? Is it because you felt them in your eyes since before the first round Moon of March appeared in your childhood?

And I give you more: a mirror in which the sky gazes at itself, a patina of grass, the drift of a butterfly, a spoonful of swallows from Chichén Itzá; a great river that flows to the rhythm of sailors and fishermen; a jingling sound of Raimundo Lulio; this heart of mine at a moment when it rejoiced, because it was being gazed upon; a green glance that went into the air and returned to infinity; the sun of sky and sound. I offer you the bottom of a dinosaur pearl, which is where you and I will live and die come three trees of years. I give you a tiny tree flower, strong and sweet. I give you the life that your parents and grandparents no longer have. I present you the smile of a great-grandmother you never knew because she was an angel and a tree and she went off to eternity in a second, with her river braids and her profile of radiant scales. I offer you a spume I found on a day I've already lost, but which we can recover in any powerful leap year. I give you my love, fugitive in the forests; I hand you half of a creature that cannot die and walks on Earth, guided by the air; I give you a horse that dreamed itself; a dew that fled from time and space to become eternal; my head freed by the wind; my soul dressed in cherry with its great ardor for adventure; I offer you an April street; a saint who vanished in the wind, a child who built himself, eye by eye and tooth by tooth, once he was given birth; a goblin who came when it went, because it didn't fear a miracle; I give you a glass full of butterflies that never sleep and always pass among bundles of trees; a woman who was suddenly lost because the air wanted her and the masculine cedars gazed upon her; and I offer you as well a woman found in the fire, whom no one could understand. I give you the ground where many flowers gather, iridescent and naked, just the way God brought them into the world; a hand outstretched between the sea and you.

Receive, Master, my endless gifts. With profound love,

Eunice Odio

P.S. — I had forgotten to offer you the entire horizon and its consequences.

June 29, 1971, Mexico

*translated by Keith Ekiss and Mauricio Espinosa*

Carlos Pellicer: Mexican poet (1897-1977). *Hora de Junio* (1937) is one of his most important collections.

## William Matthews

### *Attention, Everyone*

Gloom is the enemy, even to the end. The parodies of self-knowledge were embossed by Gloom inside our eyelids, and the abrasion makes us weep, for no reason, like a new bride disconsolate in the nightgown she had sewn so carefully. The dog comes back from the fields, lumpy with burrs. I put down my pen and pull them out; it is a care I have taught him to expect. I've always said it would be difficult.

I'm declaring a new regime. Its flag is woven loam. Its motto is: Love is worth even its own disasters. Its totem is the worm. We eat our way through grief and make it richer. We don't blunt ourselves against stones—their borders go all the way through. We go around them. In my new regime Gloom dances by itself, like a sad poet.

Also I will be sending out some letters: Dear Friends, Please come to the party for my new life. The dog will meet you at the road, barking, running stiff-legged circles. Pluck one of his burrs and follow him here. I've got lots of good wine, I'm in love, my new poems are better than my old poems. It's been too long since we started over.

The new regime will start when you lift your eyes from this page.

Here it comes.

**Steve Wilson**

## Valediction to the Reader Completing a Book of Poems

Good. You're finished. Sober with poetry, somber with reflection, make a new start of it, schooled by the images of men wandering without direction, the bell tower that houses orphans during the war, the road through the forest where light languishes on a dead leaf.

Walk out into the street with your hat in your hand. Walk out onto the promenade and greet the flower seller, the girl in the blue dress dotted with clouds, as you turn down the road to the Harbor Bridge.

Remember, all that is will pass. That the way is clear. That the moment when epiphany will transform this doorway into a sleeping beetle, this café into the carcass of the emperor's horse, is approaching. Remember, you are never and always alone.

**Amy Newman**

Editor
Sentence
Box 7 / Western Connecticut State University
181 White St.
Danbury, CT 06810

4 October

Dear Editor:

Please consider the enclosed poems for publication in *Sentence*. They are from my manuscript, *X = Pawn Capture*, a lyrical study of chess I am writing as a response assignment. The teacher said write what you know, and I thought if I had to do that, I would cry instead and miss out on the workshop discussion. Here's what I know: I know that my grandfather thought I was foolish, that my belly ached for no reason. And that when I brought out the chess pieces, and tried to polish them, it was a distraction from being a child, I was wasting some good afternoons. Why didn't I want to play like the others, awash in their apple trees, their berry bush bowls, and their bicycle races? Isolation rang in my abdomen like a sliver of ash in an eye. I clung to my grandmother's skirts and cried. The doctor came in a white stiff coat, and took the tangle out of my belly. My family stood around and waited, and when I woke up, my grandfather's body, whiter than I cold imagine, drifted close to the ceiling in fumes like a story about ether-soaked cotton. But the needles were sleek and polished, pure silver. I wish chess were clean, and free of distortion. And the words for that are in your dictionary.

Thank you for your consideration, and for reading. I have enclosed an SASE, and look forward to hearing from you.

Sincerely,
Amy Newman

## Monologue

In simple terms, a monologue is a speech. As in soliloquy, the speech may be an internal thought shared with the reader; it may or may not be literally spoken to or directed at a specific external audience. The monologue has the dual capability of revealing insight, not only into the subject being discussed by the speaker, but also into the character of the speaker him/herself. Renowned examples of monologue in poetry include Robert Browning's "My Last Duchess" and T. S. Elliot's "The Love Song of J. Alfred Prufrock."

In his poem "Ruth to Esther" Matthew Dickman uses the form of the monologue to convey the unspoken thoughts of the speaker; the poem has an epistolary feel but the language used by the speaker and the emotional impact of the last line suggest otherwise. John Ashbery's poem "A Nice Presentation" reveals the movement of a speaker's mind. The speaker is at once lucid and somewhat capricious in his monologue, similar to the ebb and flow of conversations; the reader might wonder what the subject is in the speech presented here, but by the poem's end the reader might have some sense of the content in the same way that one can get the sense of an extended conversation with multiple participants. In "Borges and I" Jorge Luis Borges uses the monologue to whimsically explore his own fractured understanding of identity. Like Borges, the speaker in Michael Palmer's "A Word Is Coming Up on the Screen..." seems to be struggling with a sense of selfhood. Whereas Borges' poem veils in subtle humor the tension created by the speaker's awareness that he is not in control, Palmer's speaker stutters out fragments of stark and arresting imagery and that suggest less ability to come to terms with chaos and chance. Finally, in the poem "Making Poison," Margaret Atwood combines the monologue with elements of anecdote, recalling a childhood experience but tinting that nostalgia with a bitter lesson.

**Matthew Dickman**

## Ruth to Esther

Why is it that when men talk about love someone always gets hurt? My breast was bitten once. Once I was only a handful. My son Obed is born and then a long string of veins go slipping through the dirt until David is born and puts on the dark. Once I heaved the barley up in the wind. Once a man found me and took me in. Once God saw me naked swimming in my skin. Why has the King of Scrolls let the calf cut up the cow? He brings on a cold front that refuses to break. Have you noticed? Esther, you're a mean beetle. Your back shines blue long into the night. Even when that night is a people who learned to gather itself together like an eyeball. You are aqueous humor, lymphy, filling the space behind the lens. I imagine you in gold chain mail, cleaning a gun. I count all my body parts and all my body parts are there. I do this when I wake up and when I go to bed. It is how I know that you are missing from me.

## John Ashbery

### A Nice Presentation

I have a friendly disposition but am forgetful, though I tend to forget only important things. Several mornings ago I was lying in my bed listening to a sound of leisurely hammering coming from a nearby building. For some reason it made me think of spring which it is. Listening I heard also a man and woman talking together. I couldn't hear very well but it seemed they were discussing the work that was being done. This made me smile, they sounded like good and dear people and I was slipping back into dreams when the phone rang. No one was there.

Some of these are perhaps people having to do with anything in the world. I wish to go away, on a dark night, to leave people and the rain behind but am too caught up in my own selfish thoughts and desires for this. For it to happen I would have to be asleep and already started on my voyage of self-discovery around the world. One is certain then to meet many people and to hear many strange things being said. I like this in a way but wish it would stop as the unexpectedness of it conflicts with my desire to revolve in a constant, deliberate motion. To drink tea from a samovar. To use chopsticks in the land of the Asiatics. To be stung by the sun's bees and have it not matter.

Most things don't matter but an old woman of my acquaintance is always predicting doom and gloom and her prophecies matter though they may never be fulfilled. That's one reason I don't worry too much but I like to tell her she is right but also wrong because what she says won't happen. Yet how can I or anyone know this? For the seasons do come round in leisurely fashion and one takes a pinch of something from each, according to one's desires and what it leaves behind. Not long ago I was in a quandary about this but now it's too late. The evening comes on and the aspens leaven its stars. It's all about this observatory a shout fills.

## Jorge Luis Borges

### Borges and I

The other one, the one called Borges, is the one things happen to. I walk through the streets of Buenos Aires and stop for a moment, perhaps mechanically now, to look at the arch of an entrance hall and the grillwork on the gate; I know of Borges from the mail and see his name on a list of professors or in a biographical dictionary. I like hourglasses, maps, eighteenth-century typography, the taste of coffee and the prose of Stevenson; he shares these preferences, but in a vain way that turns them into the attributes of an actor. It would be an exaggeration to say that ours is a hostile relationship; I live, let myself go on living, so that Borges may contrive his literature, and this literature justifies me. It is no effort for me to confess that he has achieved some valid pages, but those pages cannot save me, perhaps because what is good belongs to no one, not even him, but rather to the language and to tradition. Besides, I am destined to perish, definitively, and only some instant of myself can survive in him. Little by little, I am giving over everything to him, though I am quite aware of his perverse custom of falsifying and magnifying things. Spinoza knew that all things long to persist in their being; the stone eternally wants to bc a stone and the tiger a tiger. I shall remain in Borges, not in myself (if it is true that I am someone), but I recognize myself less in his books than in many others or in the laborious strumming of a guitar. Years ago I tried to free myself from him and went from the mythologies of the suburbs to the games with time and infinity,but those games belong to Borges now and I shall have to imagine other things.

Thus my life is a flight and I lose everything and everything belongs to oblivion, or to him.

I do not know which of us has written this page.

*translated by James E. Irby*

**Michael Palmer**

*"A word is coming up on the screen..."*

A word is coming up on the screen, give me a moment. In the meantime let me tell you a little something about myself. I was born in Passaic in a small box flying over Dresden one night, lovely figurines. Things mushroomed after that. My cat has twelve toes, like poets in Boston. Upon the microwave she sits, hairless. The children they say, you are no father but a frame, waiting for a painting. Like, who dreamed you up? Like, gag me with a spoon. Snow falls—winter. Things are aglow. One hobby is Southeast Asia, nature another. As a child I slept beneath the bed, fists balled. A face appeared at the window, then another, the same face. We skated and dropped, covering our heads as instructed. Then the music began again, its certainty intact. The true dancers floated past. They are alive to this day, as disappearing ink. After the storm we measured the shore, I grew to four feet then three. I drove a nail the page and awoke smiling. That was my first smile. In a haze we awaited the next. You said, "Antinucleons." You said, "Do not steal my words for your work." Snow falls—winter. She hands out photographs of the Union dead. Things are aglow. I traded a name for what followed it. This was useless. The palace of our house has its columns, its palms. A skull in a handcart. I removed a tongue and an arm, but this was useless. On Tuesday Freud told me, "I believe in beards and women with long hair. Do not fall in love." Is there discourse in the tropics? Does the central motif stand out clearly enough? In this name no letters repeat, so it cannot be fixed. Because it's evening I remember memory now. Your English I do not speak. A word is coming up on the screen.

## Margaret Atwood

### Making Poison

When I was five my brother and I made poison. We were living in a city then, but we probably would have made the poison anyway. We kept it in a paint can under somebody else's house and we put all the poisonous things into it that we could thing of: toadstools, dead mice, mountain ash berries which may not have been poisonous but looked it, piss which we saved up in order to add it to the paint can. By the time the can was full everything in it was very poisonous.

The problem was that once having made the poison we couldn't just leave it there. We had to do something with it. We didn't want to put it into anyone's food, but we wanted an object, a completion. There was no one we hated enough, that was the difficulty.

I can't remember what we did with the poison in the end. Did we leave it under the corner of the house, which was made of wood and brownish yellow? Did we throw it at someone, some innocuous child? We wouldn't have dared an adult. Is this a true image I have, a small face streaming with tears and red berries, the sudden knowledge that the poison was really poisonous after all? Or did we throw it out, do I remember those red berries floating down a gutter, into a culvert, am I innocent?

Whey did we make the poison in the first place? I can remember the glee with which we stirred and added, the sense of magic and accomplishment. Making poison is as much fun as making a cake. People like to make poison. If you don't understand this you will never understand anything.

## Dialogue

Dialogue is a device well known to eve[illegible] is a conversation between or among two or more [illegible]. In literature, dialogue can be a subtle but extremely e[illegible]vice for developing theme or character. In poetry the e[illegible] be a bit more understated than in drama or fiction, but w[illegible] well the technique can illuminate just as broadly.

In her poem "A Quaker Meeting in Yorba I[illegible]chel Loden uses dialogue to admit the reader to a [illegible]ical conversation between President Nixon, his family, [illegible] his grave, the grass, and even his tombstone that offe[illegible] not only into the character of the speakers but that als[illegible] the many tensions and dynamics that exist between the [illegible]nd the world they shared. Maxine Chernoff, on the oth[illegible]ses the dialogue between two speakers in her poem [illegible]ly Bodies" to plumb the depths of different philosophic[illegible]es. The tension between the speakers as they ponder the [illegible] of their existence and their mortality fluctuate[illegible]en existentialism and nihilism before ultimately al[illegible]e speakers the escape of distraction. Brian Clements'[illegible]t Date" reads like a micro-play, a brief interaction be[illegible]o characters that uses absurd dialogue and situation to c[illegible]n the absurdity of racism.

## Rachel Loden

### A Quaker Meeting in Yorba Linda

*The Richard Nixon Library & Birthplace*
*Yorba Linda, California*

The little flower of Yorba Linda told the gravestone: "Get thee behind me"

The gravestone told the grass: "I am coming out of you like a shiny tooth"

The grass asked Mrs. Nixon: "Are you dressed for Easter morning?"

Mrs. Nixon told Tricia and Julie: "Girls, your father is sprouting from the grave"

Tricia and Julie told Checkers: "You must rise too, and come away"

Checkers told us: "Why would I rise? You promised to rebury me at the Library and Birthplace. I am still here at the Bide-a-Wee Pet Cemetery in Wantagh, New York, and not one of you has ever been to visit me"

Tricia and Julie told us: "When we were little girls, we spake as little girls, we understood as little girls, we thought as little girls: but when we became Mrs. Edward Cox and Mrs. David Eisenhower, we put away childish things"

Mrs. Nixon told us: "I am Thelma Catherine Ryan, a miner's daughter and a beauty"

The grass told us: "I feel so light without that shiny stone, so green and airy"

The gravestone told us: "The little flower's death is written on my body"

The little flower of Yorba Linda told us: "I am rising even if Pat and Checkers will not rise with me. How many did we kill in Laos? Think big, for Crissakes, Henry"

I said: "Dear Friends, will you sit and quake awhile with me? I invite the gravestone, the grass, the beautiful Thelma Catherine Ryan, Mrs. Cox and Mrs. Eisenhower, Checkers sick-at-heart in Wantagh, even Henry, if he wishes, even the shy flower of Whittier, the angry flower of San Clemente, the thwarted flower of Yorba Linda"

## Maxine Chernoff

### Heavenly Bodies

—When is that huge meteor scheduled to hit Earth?
—I heard something about 2035.
—You mean in thirty-seven years the world might end?
—The world wouldn't end.
—If a meteor of that size hits Earth, we'll be destroyed.
—We might be destroyed, but there'd still be a world.
—Do you mean a universe?
—I guess that's what I mean.
—How will there be a universe if we're not there to form the concept?
—Do you think we're so important that the whole universe can't exist if we don't ? What was here before we were born?
—History was here.
—That's exactly it. We're simply a part of it all, like a whorl in a tree trunk.
—Why don't you say a grain of sand on a beach?
—How can someone who knows so much about the universe be persuaded to use a cliché?
—Death is a cliché.
—What do you mean?
—It's given to us, and we can do nothing to change it.
—But you're saying our own deaths don't matter. Not now. Not in thirty years, not if the universe gets destroyed.
—Exactly.
—So what should we do?
—About what?
—What should we do to prevent the meteor from destroying us?
—I guess we could intercept it.
—Who, you and me?

—The government.
—I knew it.
—Knew what?
—You're some kind of hired assassin.
—What do you mean?
—You're hired by the government to make me think I don't matter, not even if I die.
—How does that make me an assassin?
—It's conceptual. You erase me with your thoughts.
—So maybe I'm more of an artist than an assassin.
—How much do they pay you?
—Who?
—The government.
—Why would the government hire me to convince you of anything? Are either of us so important?
—Here you go again. You just won't admit it.
—Admit what?
—That when we die the universe will perish.
—Okay. When we die the universe will perish. Does that make you feel better?
—Yes, momentarily.

**Brian Clements**

## Elephant Date

*for Nikki Santilli*

Two elephants, Margad and Nwanda, talk over a candlelit dinner.

MARGAD

[laughing] ...oh, that is priceless!

NWANDA

[chuckling] Yes, I have to admit...

MARGAD

And he never suspected?

NWANDA

No, never!

MARGAD

Oh, me! Ah... Nwanda, this has been such a lovely evening. I hope you feel the same way...?

NWANDA

Yes... yes, Margie... may I call you Margie?

MARGAD

You may... but I love to hear you say my full name...

NWANDA

Margad.

MARGAD

Mm.

NWANDA

Margad, I can't remember having an evening like this in years.

MARGAD

Oh, that can't be true. You're so... I don't know. I'm sure you've been with many, many women.

NWANDA

No, not so! Not women like you, Margad. It almost makes me wish...

MARGAD

What? Wish what, Nwanda?

NWANDA

Surely it has occurred to you that your family might not approve of your seeing someone of my... ear size...

MARGAD

I'm trying not to think about it. I don't know what I would do if I had to choose...

NWANDA

That's very kind of you to say, Margad. But I would never come between you and your family. I couldn't disrespect them, or you, like that...

MARGAD

Nwanda. You know I am a woman of her own will.

NWANDA

Yes, yes, I know that, Margad, and that is what I love about you so...

MARGAD

Oh, Nwanda, I cannot tell you how long I've ached to here those words from your sweet, relatively small as compared to body size, well-lubricated, tusk-protected mouth...

NWANDA

Please, Margad! It drives me mad to hear that kind of talk from your beautiful, even smaller, multifunctional mouth...

MARGAD

Oh, Nwanda. Kiss me!

[they kiss]

Let's leave tonight! We'll go somewhere far away where they don't care about ear size or shoulder height...

NWANDA

[pulling away] I'm afraid no such place exists, Margad. Wherever we go we will be disgraced. But I don't care. I love you. I love you!

[they kiss again, then, joining trunks, they stampede the restaurant and smash out the door]

## Hybrid Poems

The term "hybrid poem" describes a work that incorporates conventions from more than one genre. The possibilities for such work are as endless as the differing forms, genres, and media that could be thrown together. The singular requirement of the hybrid poem is that it employs the chosen forms or genres in such a manner as to utilize their initial strengths, while at the same time realizing some new intensity from the collaboration.

In his haibun-like poem "In the Shop," poet James Merrill breaks from two paragraphs of prose with three lines of verse. The transition is somewhat abrupt but works startlingly well. The verse functions not so much to change the style of the writing but to slow down the words and punctuate their meaning with white space. "03.03.03" by Amjad Nasser is constructed around a day and leaps from journalistic prose to short lines that function like flash poetry and back again. The resulting combination of observation, cultural reference, and imagination remind us that we're never far from disturbing and threatening violence. Steve Myers inverts and adapts the haibun form to a more contemporary use in his "Haibun for Smoke and Fog."

## James Merrill

### In The Shop

Out came the most fabulous kimono of all; dark, dark purple traversed by a winding, starry path. To what function, dear heart, could it possibly be worn by the like of—

Hush. Give me your hand. Our trip has ended, our quarrel was made up. Why couldn't the rest be?

Dyeing. A homophone deepens the trope. Surrendering to Earth's colors, shall we no be Earth before we know it? Venerated therefore is the skill which, prior to immersion, inflicts upon sacrificial length of crepe de Chine certain intricate knottings no hue can touch. So that one fine day, painstakingly unbound, this terminal gooseflesh, the fable's whole eccentric

star-puckered moral—
white, never-to-blossom buds
of the mountain laurel—

may read as having emerged triumphant from the vats of night.

## Amjad Nasser

03.03.03

This day, in which a bearded man of Middle Eastern mien exhorted an English girl not to take the metro, in which she handed him his wallet, which had slipped to the ground when he was about to leave the cab, has gone by slowly.

The three-zeroed-threes—blind date with the Devil's Machine—is but another slow-witted and numerically evil portent.

Nevertheless, as the Hammersmith Municipality Electronic sign on King Street points out, this day is another ordinary London day.

Daylight here is shorter than Arabian delight.

The temperature is 11 degrees Celsius.

And the sky, such as there is, is a dome of ashes.

Kings Mall's automatic gates open and close like a terrified eyelid.

Policemen—with their black costumes and pointed hats as if they had stepped out of cheap tourism postcards—are leading away a homeless drunkard who was about to piss on the River Island Boutique.

A bored traffic guard is writing out a ticket for a 1970's Volkswagen van, emblazoned with the bold letters: NO WAR. It seems it has been parked on a yellow line.

Monday, 03.03.03,
(The third day of the Arabian week also)
Is another ordinary London day.
I did not fall in love.
The traffic hasn't changed from right to left.
Osama Bin Laden did not strike again.
The Palestinians on Curry's TV screen are engaged in
Their usual pantomimic death.
Bush and Blair are vying with each other to see who
Can be the most vicious of all.
The world, as Wallace Stevens says, is ugly and
People are sad.

*translated by Leonard Schwartz and Tahseen al Khateeb*

**Steve Myers**

## Haibun for Smoke and Fog

My father liked a bad joke
with a Japanese prisoner
over a makeshift fire
better than his own barrack.

He never spoke
of the celebrated
Daibutsu Buddha.

New Year after the Emperor's surrender, on the Nara to Osaka train. My father strikes up a conversation, in pidgin, with a Japanese couple, smokes cigarettes with them, jokes with their little boy. Hands him a chocolate bar like he's bucking for "B" battery's Good Samaritan Medal. God knows he's grateful there was no landing, as planned, on southern Honshu, with him on the front line and 90 per cent casualties a "given." Nineteen at the time, he only wants to go home to York, Pennsylvania, teach high school history, watch Laurel and Hardy at the Saturday matinee. He believes in the Emerson Emerson would have him believe, and as luck would have it, is one of the few GIs in the 368th Field Artillery who wouldn't have a go with her when the husband grins and says to him "My wifu... you pom-pom," grinding his right fist in his left hand so my father cannot take his meaning wrong.

*

Spring thaw after snow;
bloodroot, then blacksnake,
then fire azalea
on the forest floor.

The snake, notoriously, does not blink, and neither, in "The Fog of War," does Robert McNamara, who once ordered Japan more horizon than it had seen since the Tokugawa shoguns. Basho's time—all the industrial cities went widescreen in the firestorm. Not even Dresden suffered such spot-on efficiency from the B-29s, their magnesium incendiary bombs and, in the full Technicolor of its first coming, napalm. Among the Pfc.—my father's Nippon hand-me-downs, this after-photo of Osaka; call it "Column, Rubble, Sky."

*

The temple city
a last vertical
steel column;
my eye unreels
its plumbline
down, adjusts
its spirit level.

By the last Sixties, The Secretary had become a pair of wire rims and lacquered hair behind a podium. My girlfriend's fiancé was already in 'Nam then, a flyer whose lifespan was measured in minutes. Beyond her 17 years she was practical, self-reliant, knew before anyone we were in for a long war, made all the necessary adjustments. One sweltering summer evening we lay down in a thicket of speargrass and, after, read his description of fuel oil burning on the Mekong River, seen from the air. This time it was me that started crying. I was thinking of my father, how he worked double-time to take my mind off Cronkite and my lottery number, one night calling me into our darkened kitchen, where he struck a match and touched it to the border of our nineteenth-century porcelain sink. He's written my name there, with flourishes, in lighter fluid, before the flame.

## "Free-Line" Poems

Poet Sally Ashton coined the label "free-line poem" to refer to poems that inhabit a kind of half-way point between prose poem and free verse. These poems use the sentence *as* the line—that is, each line of the poem is a sentence (or a near-sentence fragment). Says Ashton in *Sentence 2*: "With free-line form, the construction varies from poet to poet but generally consists of stand-alone sentences running margin to margin and separated by a skipped line. It's as if stanzas compromised of one sentence made up the poem. The skipped line's empty space achieves a momentary stillness, like an exhaled breath, between sentences."

In Ashton's conception, as demonstrated here in her poem "Origins of Sublime," no line is dependent upon previous or subsequent lines in order to "belong," so they frequently have a sense of the collage. Marvin Bell's "Dead Man" poems have a similar feel of lines collected, but the poems tend to have more association from line to line and tend to build toward an implied narrative. At times these poems by Bell are similar in structure to some of Walt Whitman's more prosaic poems. Alan Sondheim uses the sentence-line in "Origin of Poetry" as syntactic unit and sound unit, building a hypnotic rhythm which perfectly reinforces the poem's point about poetry's foundation.

## Sally Ashton

### Origins of Sublime

—A foreshortened arm, a breast, a cage of pigeons built from sticks.
—So we're dying or something.
—It's the "something" that I'm interested in, shiny as new money or water's perfect coin.
—You're the kind of girl taxi drivers make faces at.
—I'm the kind of girl who watches one bird sail in open sky, who sips tea in the airport and notices your movements, your luggage.
—What about that stack of severed heads nearby, the tongues blackened, blood puddled?
—That kind of girl, too.
—A girl who sweats great circles under her arms. Who are you actually talking to?
—I was not happy and today I became happy.
—Don't forget how an old man warms his back in the sun.
—Ink dribbles down my chin and stains my lips.
—An old man in the sun and his thoughts pulled low like a hat, the brim disguising his eyes.
—Out there great gray bodies twist in the sea.
—He leans and watches the children play soccer while shadows lengthen.
—All undiscovered the place where it rains, or where great bodies dive and moan.
—Quiet as the casks where grapes dream.
—You open your eyes to the same room and sun drifts simple shafts across the bed.
—Everything going fast like a ripe tomato with a split in its side.

—Rain in the alley, on the air conditioner. Clean streets, wet garbage.

—That kind.

—Our lot narrow and deep.

—Each night the stars burn like whiskey, blurred like a headache.

—I've found what seems a silence holds traffic hum, voices calling, the smell of supper cooking, someone scuffing their feet.

—And the slapping sound of sex.

—The scrape of insect wings, the exhalation of breath.

## Marvin Bell

from *The Book of the Dead Man*

1. About the Beginnings of the Dead Man

When the dead man throws up, he thinks he see his inner life.
Seeing his vomit, the thinks he sees his inner life.
Now he can pick himself apart, weigh the ingredients, research
his makeup.
He wants to study things outside himself if he can find them.
Moving, the dead man makes the sound of bone on bone.
He bends a knee that doesn't wish to bend, he raises an arm that
argues with a shoulder, he turns his head by throwing it
wildly to the side.
He envies the lobster the protective sleeves of its limbs.
He believes the jellyfish has it easy, floating, letting everything
pass through it.
He would like to be starfish, admired for its shape long after.
Everything the dead man said, he now takes back.
Not as a lively young demonstrates sincerity or regret.
A young dead man and an old dead man are two different things.
A young dead man is oil, an old dead man is water.
A young dead man is bread and butter an old dead man is bread
and water—it's a difference in construction, also
architecture.
The dead man was there in the beginning: to the dead man, the
sky is a crucible.
In the dead man's lifetime, the planet has changed from lava to
ash to cement.
But the dead man flops his feathers, he brings his wings up over
his head and has them touch, he bends over with his beak

to the floor, he folds and unfolds at the line where his armor creases.
The dead man is open to change and has deep pockets.
The dead man is the only one who will live forever.

2. More About the Beginnings of the Dead Man

One day the dead man looked up and saw the sun.
The dead man in those days held the sky like a small globe, like a patchwork ball, like an ultramarine bowl.
The man softened it, kneaded it, turned it and gave it volume.
He thrust a hand deep into it and shaped it from the inside out.
He blew into it and pulled it and stretched it until it became full-sized, a work of art created by a dead man.
The excellence of it, the quality, its character, its fundamental nature, its *raison d'être*, its "it" were all indebted to the dead man.

The dead man is the flywheel of the spinning planet.
The dead man thinks he can keep things the same by not moving.
By not moving, the dead man maintains the status quo at the center of change.
The dead man, by not moving, is an explorer: he follows his nose.
When it's not personal, not profound, he can make a new world anytime.
The dead man is the future, was always the future, can never be the past.
Like God, the dead man existed before the beginning, a time marked by galactic static.
Now nothing remains of the first static that isn't music, fashioned into melody by the accidents of interval.
Now nothing more remains of silence that isn't sound.
The dead man has both in the past and his head in the clouds.

## Alan Sondheim

### Origin of Poetry

First the owner George Steinbrenner came to mind.
I couldn't remember the name of the manager.
I tried and tried and thought, if I didn't want to remember it, I would.
Over and over again, and then a rhythm came to my mind.
It was dah dah di, dah dah di.
I knew it was connected with the name.
Joe Torre, or Torres, that was the name I was thinking of.
But first, it was the incantation, dah dah di, that rhythm.
The rhythm appeared before the name, incantatory.
I thought this is similar to the condition of pausological constructs.
For example, "This is what I wanted to do, but {pause} ..."
The pause is after the conjunction.
The structure is already fulfilled.
It's the same with incantation, the structure is there.
(The structure which is always there beforehand.)
Or rhyme, the structure is there. Alliteration.
But the incantatory preceded the name, the name a singularity.
Connected with the choratic rhythm of the body.
Disconnected momentarily with the name.
Establishing the rhythm of the name.
Establishing the name as a placeholder of the name.
A placeholder of the name that was generated by the name.
Or generated by the sound or the rigid designator of structure.
Rigid designator of structure and placeholder intertwined.
The intermeshing of primordial impulse.
Primordial in the sense of gesture and incantatory gesture.
Incantation is gesture, gesture incantation.

Every word tends towards others of its kind.
Poetry of incantation, weight of language, predecessor of name.
The moment of the name in incantation.
The call of Joe Torre in the primordial rhythm of the name.
The sounding of Joe Torre and the world.

## Structural Analogues

Many of the other sections in this book are actually subsets of this category. In strategies such as the list poem, aphorism, fable, and monologue, the prose poem takes on the structural conventions of other discourses. This strategy is not unique to prose poems. Critic Jonathan Holden has argued that this strategy is characteristic of postmodern American poetry. From this perspective, the recent popularity of the prose poem might be attributable to its very ability to absorb such a wide range of discourses.

Paul Violi's "Triptych" takes on the structure of a *TV Guide* listing as an imaginative way of listing some of the seemingly chaotic elements of Western culture, some of which might come into play on a daily basis for a contemporary citizen and some, ironically, not. John Richards's "Ethics Case Book of the American Psychiatric Association" takes on the skeletal structure of the actual case book of that title in order to meditate on ethics in the psychoanalytic environment. Tom Andrews uses the conventions of the screenplay to hilarious effect in his "Cinéma Verité" poems.

Other prose poets have taken on received verse forms such as sonnets and sestinas as models. Janet Kaplan and Kathleen Kirk, for example, take slightly different approaches to using the sonnet's 14-line paradigm to structure their prose poems.

The concrete poem is really something other than a prose poem or a verse poem, but we have included in this section examples of concrete poetry—Theo Hummer's "Moravia: Postcards," Irving Weiss's "Eight," and Gavin Selerie's "Casement"—that employ prose or other organizations of language that lean toward prose poetry in mood and appearance.

**Theo Hummer**

## Moravia: Postcards

She arrives in the season of drifting spiderwebs, of mealy purplish apples, of young wine a graying wolf-eyed student brings in plastic pop bottles from his own vineyard. It tastes like Kool-aid, a glass makes her dizzy. She leaves the bottles capped and in a week one explodes, coating the furnished room's surfaces with mauve foam. The rest go to the dumpster, wasted on her. This is not to say she finds no magic here—for example, her native tongue is straw, in this country, that can be spun to gold. She teaches in the local factory. Days off, she takes

The bus to Brno—it stops at every village newsstand: cigarettes and chocolate, the two national newspapers, a stunning array of pornography. Knickered weekenders from Vienna, coppery pheasants slung from their belts, prowl the flax-fields in twos and threes—storybook Huntsmen—she's a child again: pantomimes in the gas station, too shy to use her words, can't go to the doctor or bank alone. Mirror-practices before her big transaction: *Six postcard stamps to America, please. Express.* Or: *I would like two hectograms of cheese.* The town is too small to give foreigners language lessons. She learns to speak, nights, with the factory translator's two-year-old. In this way her vocabulary comes to include the words for *lollipop, duckie,* and *poo.* The translator asks when she will think of marriage—the once she has a date, he says *Love is a great beautifier.* Or else she studies alone: grammar, menus and bus schedules. Or else, by rote and repetition, *beer* and swear words at the pub from men her age who live with their parents. Jobs are scarce for the young, and she is lucky in her own place! with 13

TV channels! even one—CNN—in English. She keeps it on for company, by evening can recite its 15-minute global newsreels, comfortingly banal compared with what has happened not twenty miles from here: teenage girls with lilacs for the Red Army; Napoleon at Austerlitz; the Hussite wars, protestant blood before Luther's birth. Perhaps her hackles rise in villages still equipped with loudspeakers right out of some Second World War movie—she reads the condensed histories in *Fodor's* to scare herself, pictures other trains than these where she can buy a Coke or stretch across three seats to nap—but really, what can she feel or imagine? The young men from the pub were thirteen when the curtain lifted, claim, *we remember nothing.* Their parents have no English. She hears thirdhand that people are nostalgic for the old days, though her factory students haltingly describe, when pressed to say what it was like, lines stretching around the block for oranges at Christmas—then

fall silent. The sky grows darker day by day, and then there's snow. The roads and villages are mute—or she is deaf—or both. *What was here?* Ghost among ghosts, she passes through, not touching or being touched: these words, after all—her only currency—are utterly devalued: where can she spend them? And whose story can she understand or tell, except her own? She's alone, a prelingual being, innocent and selfish.

## Gavin Selerie

### Casement

Could not be called a cave. Dark and bright the stones. United by labour. A vaulted passage with many stairs. Reft of reach. Sunbeams strain through painted glass. Friend is the voice carried by holes in a statue. Family covers forbidden issue. Echoes with the lightest foot. A song can dilate the heart while passion still hid.

Black velvet den under azure seal winding wormly away from what is fled the world. Half hallowed to reflower. Ghouls slip between self and relation, she goes ruin strewn to the summons (such a guardian as wolf to lamb). Why style a safe home a prison?

Can't get out and if you do there is another version. Appear singular as story fractures rambling against fact. White turns to cream—week, month, year. All figments partake of tunneled ore: ciphers, sonnets, ringlets of hair. Whether to skirt no is our refrain.

Must our hearts throb before inanimate canvas? Who in a castle was kept a princely guest like jewels secure. The door so often sought is that portrait deftly sprung in the flickering murk. Seen without being known as lost and when marked ready to vent this space. Again letters betray. Residua cleave to the rendered casket.

**Paul Violi**

Triptych

\-------------------

MORNING

\-------------------

6:30 (2) Sunrise
(4) Knowledge
(5) Comparative Geography
(13) Images and Things
(71) Listen and Learn
7:00 (2) News
(4) News
(5) WIDE WORLD
(8) Public Affairs
7:30 (4) Young Africans
(9) Elsie Aquacade The Young and the Restless
(13) Religious Humoresque
(71) Espionage
8:00 (2) Asian Dimension
(5) To Be Announced
(6) Vanishing Point
A Sentinel in Swamplight;
snow falling
on black mud.
(10) WEATHER.
Flood footage,
birds hop
from branch to
branch as the
water rises
higher
and higher.
8:30 (8) PERIPLUM
(9) Mr. Itchy Starlight
(11) DUENDE. He
drives into a
tree,
he listens to the
apples bounce
off the hood
of his car.
8:45 (9) WEATHER.
Thunder claps,
the clouds
stampede.
(10) SUBMISSION

9:00 (2) Bugs Bunny
(7) Snorkeling with Captain Bravo
(8) TALES. "Why all this fear and trembling?" said the Wizard to the Shrew. "Is life all you know?"
9:30 (80) Violence in Blue
(4) Lisping Marauder
(71) El Reporter
10:00 (7) SERMON. What part of paradise is made of memory.
(9) SCIENCE. A hammock Rope is tied around a tree; as the trunk grows the bark swallows the rope and leaves an interesting scar.
10:30 (13) MODERN EXPLOR-ATION. The space a seemingly mindless rush hour crowd leaves around a raving idiot.
(71) BLINDSPOT
11:00 (2) FANFARE. Blood on a concrete piano.
(4) LOVELORN. Figure on a mountaintop digging up seashells.
(5) Dragonquest
(7) Elizabethan and Nova Scotian Music (with Charles North).
11:30 (9) FEATURE. Telling fortunes by burning seaweed.
(13) MUTINY. Fog drifts up to the house and crashes through the windows. Elephants

bark in the
distance.
(71) FUTURAMA

-----------------

AFTERNOON

--------------------------

12:00 (4) News
(7) NEWS AND WEATHER. The weather hunting silence.
(8) INQUISITION
12:30 (2) A CHILLING TALE. A man with long blonde hair hands a threatening note to a teller with long blonde hair.
(13) MODERN EXPLOR-ATION. A deer trying to climb a ladder.
(71) NECROPOLIS
(6) INTERLUDE. Poisoned rats not in the walls. You vacuum large black flies off the screens.
1:00 (5) WHITE STRAW-BERRIES
(7) SNORT. No war buff, me.
(8) Damaged Perspective
(9) APPLIANCES AT AN EXHIBITION
(10) Smut
1:30 (6) TIME SPAN. "...and the spiders were singing in the wells."
(71) SCIENCE. An examination into the earwax of various races. Curious results.
(80) WEATHER. Bleak snowlight, black

helicopters
to the rescue.
1:45 (4) Dream
Overload
(5) A stack of
Bibles
2:00 (2) VIGIL. 8
people on a
train platform
reading
little books.
(4) DISCOVERY.
My elbow, the
left one,
the first time
I've noticed it
in years.
Highlights:
scars from
unremembered
wounds, new
hair.
(5) Polythemus
(13) LA
HISTORIA.
The men in
Columbus'
crew are
allotted over
two liters of red
wine per diem.
2:30 (6) Mostly Prose.
A bug
flies through
my eye.
The crowd
cheers.
(8) CHERISHED
FORMS
3:00 (7) Conquistador
(13) MODERN
EXPLOR-
ATION.
Spaces in the
air where the
wind waits
disguised
as silence.
4:00 (4) JUMPING
JESUS
(5) Split Second
4:30 (6) VANISHING
POINT.
And I sink
through
the chilly rain
and leafless
trees past
the colorful
clothes left out
on the line.
(8) SPORTS
AND
WEATHER.
Click. clunk.
people
bowling in the
fog.

5:00 (2) HOMILY.
A long
lost color
returns
to earth in a
fleet of
clouds, ending
millennia of
heretofore
inexplicable
melancholia.
(9) BITCH
ON WHEELS
6:00 (2) Hitleresque
(13) ARCHAE-
OLOGY.
Pillars strewn
wowiezowie
across the sea
floor of a
sunken
palladium.
(71) RALPH
WONDERFUL
(80) Bucharest
7:00 (2) News
(4) Cow with a
hair-lip:
Moof.
(7) NEWS AND
WEATHER.
Intermittent
gales
which drown
the crickets,
hundreds
of acorns hit
the roof and
roll down
the shingles.

----------------

Evening

----------------

7:30 (13) Brahms. Piano
Concerto 2 in B
flat major.
(45) Pythagoras
8:00 (2) UPDATE. The
magicians
explain
why they
failed.
(9) SOUVENIR.
A pubic hair,
a perfect 6, on
a bar of soap.
9:00 (7) Art which was
not interested
in motion or
time.
(9) HOUR
OF BLISS
(11) STRANGE
ENCOUNTER.
"Neither
darkness

nor light,"
said the
Swamp Angel,
"Neither
darkness
nor light can
fill my eyes."
10:00 (2) CUISINE. Does
torn bread
really
taste better than
sliced bread?
(8) Black Dimes
10:30 (7) MY BLOOD
RAN COLD
(9) The Young
Elpenor.
Besotted, he
falls off roof,
breaks neck,
dies. The
sea-dark wine.
(11) KARMA.
The live,
leafless
branches
and the dead
tree against the
sky, all
grappling with
the wind.
(71) TIME AND
TOLERANCE.
An invisible
nude enters the
elevator.
She's chewing
gum.
11:00 (2) Moon out of
focus.
(5) INTER-
MISSION.
She leaves the
table, her
elbows are wet.
(6) Cloud Armada
(8) Hours bubbling
in the ever-
lasting wake of
Paradise.
(11) CANYON.
Another
herd faceless
and innum-
erable rushes
by without
showing
Biff and Sally
the way out.
11:30 (5) WAVES
wearing
warbonnets
charge a pair of
plump identical
twins.
(6) FIFI FLEES—
FOUL PLAY
FEARED.

(8) TYPICAL
BAUDE-
LAIRE:
"...no point is
sharper than
that of the
infinite."

12:00 (2) LUMINARY.
In 1903, he
turned
his attention to
the east...

(9) WATERLOO.
Napolean loses
because severe
case of
hemorrhoids
prevents him
from
concentrating
on the course
of the battle.

(11) FINISHING
TOUCHES.
A cloud floats
up to the moon
and stops.
Jolting finale
avoided.

## John Richards

### Ethics Case Book of the American Psychoanalytic Association

I. PRINCIPLES AND STANDARDS OF ETHICS FOR PSYCHOANALYSTS

Begin inquiries with reflections from a lost mirror.
Swim only in narrow estuaries.
At times choice will be difficult.
The encyclopedia of the child will be left open at the last
page.
Acquire bifocals. Limit principles.

II. PROVISIONS FOR THE IMPLEMENTATION OF THE PRINCIPLES AND STANDARDS OF ETHICS FOR PSYCHOANALYSTS

Procedures.

III. INTRODUCTION TO THE AMERICAN PSYCHO-ANALITIC ASSOCATION CASE BOOK

Dependent variables begin to emerge.
"Techniques once seen as acceptable may be considered
unethical by current standards."
Differentials compromise each approach.
"Attitudes, behaviors and interactions which might have
been seen as violations of proper technique years ago
may, in today's theoretical pluralism, be viewed as
acceptable."
We continue to misplace our century.

## IV. CASE VIGNETTES AND DISCUSSION OF ISSUES IN APPLYING PRINCIPLES OF ETHICS TO CLINICAL PRACTICE

### A. PSYCHOANALITICAL COMPETENCE

The psychiatrist commits suicide.
His patients begin to see an improvement in his therapeutic technique.
His colleagues erupt into vigorous debate.
Is resurrection an accepted form for his scandalous behavior?

### B. CONFIDENTIALITY

A doctor tells the same joke over and over again.
Are we legally obliged to report the anxiety and shame?

### C. RELATIONSHIPS WITH COLLEAGUES, STUDENTS AND SUPERVISEES

Participating in cliques. Gossiping.
Building a following among colleagues.
Theoretical differences.
Compatible and pleasurable evenings together posing the severest ethical dilemmas.
We are such little gods.

### D. ETHICAL VS. TECHNICAL VIOLATIONS

The patient suffers an infarction.
His analyst faces the void.
Our theories provoke rationalization.
Our violations provide.

## E. SAFEGUARDING THE PUBLIC AND PROFESSION

Her mother loved the brother best.
We observe the isolated self.
The analyst takes her hand.
Counter transference feelings become difficult for each of us.
We search for the private murderers among ourselves.

## F. AVOIDING EXPLOITATION

### 1. SEXUAL BOUNDARY ISSUES

The patient rises from the couch.
The analyst embraces her.
They look out the window together.
The long phase of erotic tension gives way to the long phase of erotic tension.
She accuses him of making multiple mistakes.
He writes a six page single spaced letter.
His erotic dream was a form of boundary crossing.

### 2. NON-SEXUAL BOUNDARY ISSUES

The patient rises from the couch.
The analyst does not embrace her.
They look out the window together.
All boundaries are sexual.

G. IMPLEMENTING THE CODE

Rumors are circulating.
The love-sick analyst.
He has kissed her.
Sex again.
We stretch him out on the table. We spread his arms.

## Tom Andrews

*Cinéma Verité: The Death of Alfred, Lord Tennyson*

The camera pans a gorgeous snow-filled landscape: rolling hills, large black trees, a frozen river. The snow falls and falls. The camera stops to find Tennyson, in an armchair, in the middle of a snowy field.

Tennyson:

It's snowing. The snow is like… the snow is like crushed aspirin,
like bits of paper…, no, it's like gauze bandages, clean teeth,
shoelaces, headlights… no,
I'm getting too old for this, it's like a huge T-shirt that's been
chewed on by a dog.
it's like semen, confetti, chalk, sea shells, woodsmoke, ash, soap,
trillium, solitude, daydreaming… Oh hell,
you can see for yourself! That's what I hate about film!

He dies.

## Janet Kaplan

### Fourteen Lines

*...I will put Chaos into fourteen lines*
*And keep him there; and let him thence escape*
*If he be lucky...*
*-Edna St. Vincent Millay*

1.
Chaos and Order shared a house of lines.

2.
Chaos woke early to play with his toys.
(He'd taught then to say "Order!") "What a grand
Day it is," said Chaos, irregular
Prose breaking steadily through the blinds.

3.
Order gave Chaos a playful kick.
Then they shouldered their grenades and leapt off
Into the world's strict confines.

4.
They were trying hard not to seem little, dressed in black and smoking cigarettes. Order wore a tracking device.

5.
The human hiding in the pantry began to write a sonnet but the shape led to a clean slate.

6.
It would be easy to think I hadn't wanted to write a sonnet. Or that I lacked its abiding faith.

7.
Art had a face, but the soul did not. I pulled art's hair out. What would save me from hedonism and morality, my utilitarian masks?

8.
Chaos sent ruined sonnets, a rude sort of gift. Nothing more than the fierce blankness which, in times of war, overcomes me at my task.

9.
There was a switch stuck in transit, which meant the train couldn't move. Someone said, "It's a Code-Orange train," meaning a homeland squad was giving us the once-over.

10.
Fourteen lines with fewer cares than raindrops
About to be devoured by a rose.

11.
Sonnet: "little sound."
Un pacchetto di sigarette,
Per piacere. Senza filtro.

12.
Chaos likes to make sounds: tre     ssssh     sou     orre     cchio
Order wants     timpano     Half-widths of rabbeted keel
little rabbit fear

13.

"Of course, things do not always go perfectly when making these variations. For example, Variation 3 indicates what can occur if an x'j exists for which there is no xi>x'j... This is not a problem. When such instances occur, pitches can be inserted by the musician to preserve musical continuity, or the pitches of the original piece can be substituted."

—D.S. Dabby, "Musical variations from a chaotic mapping," Chaos 6(2), 1996.

14.

There was a little Chaos, an orderly little Chaos, stuck in transit, by which they meant the train couldn't move. "May the rest of your ride be uneventful," said the trainman, as finally home we lurched.

## Irving Weiss

### Eight

| | | | | | | | |
|---|---|---|---|---|---|---|---|
| Wait, | mate: | Fate's | grating | gates<br>late | annihi-<br>tate | precipi- | bait. |
| Termi-<br>nate | immode-<br>rate | rate. | Decela-<br>rate | indiscri-<br>miniate | gait. | Initiate | self-<br>debate. |
| Regu-<br>late | estate, | culti-<br>vate | sedate | traits, | abdi-<br>cate | irate | hate! |
| Calcu-<br>late, | mate: | Fate | denomi-<br>nates, | invali-<br>dates, | assasi-<br>nates— | capitu-<br>late | state! |
| Accom-<br>modate, | mate: | belate | date; | medi-<br>tate, | medi-<br>ate, | circu-<br>late | self-<br>extri-<br>cate. |
| Inno-<br>vate, | stimu-<br>late, | reju-<br>venate. | Suffo-<br>cate | pontifi-<br>cating | prat-<br>ings: | radiate, | illumi-<br>nate! |
| Abomi-<br>nate | degene-<br>rate | candi-<br>dates, | venerate | culti-<br>vated | magi-<br>strates: | educate, | antici-<br>pate. |
| Great | Laureate | Mate! | Plait | pate—<br>brate, | cele-<br>tulate, | congra- | fete! |

## Kathleen Kirk

### Prose Sonnet to the Silent Father

1. I won't know what to say in my next letter, since you have not answered the last and the one before.
2. I see you in every man who leans back in his chair, quiet until he's ready to push into a pause a statement like, "That's a terrible question," about the one I just asked.
3. My husband sat crying in his chair, I want to tell you, while I sang in the other room and our daughter screamed, "Stop singing!"
4. He cried for his own father, left behind in Cuba, who played the piano.
5. "because he didn't get to hear his papi sing," my daughter tells me later, "and he was still sad even with me sitting in his lap.
6. "Next time will you let me sing?"
7. 
8. Here is a letter I have revised and torn to pieces, an action you will call clichéd and sentimental.
9. You are like a poetry teacher.
10. I need to learn how to say the opposite of what I mean but without irony
11. (a prose tactic, yours).
12. I need to learn how to leave silence at the center
13. and still be able to sign my name to it
14. as if it were written by me.

# Abecedarian

The abecedarian poem uses the alphabet as an organizing principle, and the poems collected in this section demonstrate several different approaches. Andrew Neuendorf uses the sequence of the alphabet to generate the sequence of words in a long, multi-paragraphed poem that runs through the alphabetic sequence a dozen times. Similarly, Cheryl Pallant's "Yonder Zongs" cycles through the alphabet several times over with the added challenge of reducing the string by one letter with each sentence. Christian Bök's *Eunoia* is a five-chapter sequence in which every chapter uses a single vowel exclusively. We've reproduced the first poem of the "A" and "E" chapters here.

Like other poetic games or operations, the abecedarian poem can absolve the poet of the necessity of generating some structural elements of the poem so that she can focus on what is happening within the structure. One might think that such seemingly deterministic methods would overbear creativity in these poems, but the outcome can be quite the opposite and widely variant—something as virtuosic and musically amazing as Bök's work or something as politically charged as Neuendorf's poem.

**Andrew Neuendorf**

*An American Blue Comrade's Didactic Evisceration Flaming George's Geopolitical Havens, Hopefully Igniting Jabberwocky Jihad....*

Alaskans believe cacti degrade Earth's fertility. Georgia, Hell's incisor, jails Ketamine lackeys. Meanwhile, Massachusetts, never ostracizing penitent queers, rejoices same-sex twosomes usually vilified. Wyoming, xenophobic, yesteryear's zeitgeist,

auspiciously bred Cheney, denied euphemisms for greedy Halliburton infractions, jihad keepsakes, loutish multi-millionaires negotiating oil profits, quintessentially raping sacred soil, Texas unblushingly victorious, wielding XL yank-hating zealotry,

although Austin, bluesy city, differs enormously from George. Hawaii is Japan's kamikaze karmic keepsake, loving Maui-Wowie, next-door neighbor's ocean Pacific paradox: Pioneering Puritans' quixotic ruckus spoiled this tiny utopia. Virginia wishes Xmas yeoman zip

after 'baccy captured daringly downwind. Even Florida's growth-happy housing industry invalidates Jewish Justice (kaddish kibosh), kindling Kulturkampf. Little Miss Nebraska's not ostensibly prejudiced, previewing pollyannaish platitudes: "People, practice peace! Pretty please? Quiet rowdy riots. Save some sturgeon species scientists say suffer scale sickness seeping sewage spreads." Tennessee ungratefully volunteers vitriol, vulgar, way-off xenodiagnosis. Yet, Zen acrobats balance Benzedrine blues beside bed-and-breakfast Buddahood bliss, courting California's cross-legged, conscientious coastal college Christ Consciousness cravers. Connecticut's coming, cautiously, defending equality from gay-hating inbreeders, jeremiad-jabbering Klansman. Likewise, Let's laud Maryland (maybe Marryland?), Minnesota, (Mainly Minneapolis), Michigan (Michael Moore's mainland), Maine (Mmmm, maple), McGreevy's New Jersey, niche New Hampshire, Out-there Oregon, Pennsylvanian Quakers, quickly, realizing, regretfully, regressive religious retreads recently restricted rights, stymieing such states. Still, these unattached voters willfully whacked W, x-raying y'all's yodeling yokel zealot:

Adolf Bush. But, blind 'Bama boys, bound by biblical bastardizations, believe boys can't date Eric, fuck freely, find God's holy infinite jackpot kept latently, like Louisiana's Laissez-Faire logic lost 'longside mud-faced Mississippi's neo-Nazi obfuscation problem. Queens recite randy rainbow secrets, so sore, still soaring softly, swinging toward upstate Vermont, Western Washington, where women woo women without worrying whether war-lording Xaviers, yoking Zephyrus's

apocalyptic breeze, could cast-off cool cats, calling Coors' Colorado, Catholic Cleveland, Caustic Cincinnati, Carolina's crabby coastal cities (Do evangelicals even feel?) for grassroots gospel grandstanding (galvanizing gay-basher's gall). Hitler's hiding in Indiana, in Idaho, in ill-bred, inch-high Iowa, its innocence irrevocably imploding in Iraq. *Johnson, Kennedy, King, Kissinger, Lenin, Lennon, Le Duc Tho, McNamara, My Lai Massacre, Nagasaki, Nixon's Orwellian Offspring, OJ., Osama, Oswald, Ozzy Osborne, Powell, Preemptive, Potato, Quayle, Ray, Reagan, Rice, Rumsfeld squeezing Saddam's sweaty shake, Schwarzkopf, The Tonkin Truth, Trump, Truman, Unilateral,*

*Vietnam, WMDs, Wolf Blitzer, Wolfowitz, Woodstock, X-factored yin-yang zillionaires.*

Awestruck Arizona allows an ailing AIDS-afflicted actor a bedridden blunt, but backs Bush copiously despite draconian drug decrees enlightened Europeans find fascist, facile, fucked-up. Grass-growers grow good Ganja, however, in Illinois, John Kerry's lovers, Lincoln's logs made matchsticks, now Obama's progressive principality. Question Rhode Island's sanity? That undersized varmint voted with Wisconsin's woodsmen, x-cons, yellow yen-shee yak-herders zagging

away before Bush convinces Delaware Dubya's everyone's friend. God, Glowing Giver, Grant Glorious Gnosis: How ill is Jefferson, Kansas? Last Monday night online, President Puritan's quack Right-wing soldiers telegraphed tautology to ten trillion teetotalist teenyboppers, televangelist troubadours, transparent toddler-toting Toyota telemarketing tarts that tug their transplanted tits, traditional tight-ass terrorist-torturing troops, Uber-unctuous undeclared undergraduates, upchucking, unyieldingly upholding unsupportable utopian utterances urging usurpation, utilizing Utah's underground Usenet, username: UglyUrchin. Ultimately, vain, vacuous vision validates W's Xanadu. Yet, you, yawning youth, yesterday's yippie yogic Yeatsian, yield yonder zygote,

a bastardly beauty born. Contrarily, D-day eludes earnest eagles forever. Families force goodwill gifts, having ignored inspiration, jamming Kentucky's limber mandolin maligned. Missouri, Montana, Nevada, New Mexico, North Dakota, Oklahoma—Prepare! Presently, pissed-off principled people qualmishly reject Republican sanctimony. South Dakota, stop the utterly vaccinated vacationers viewing Washington's walkover warlords, Wall Drug, whatever warmed-over, wall-to-wall white bread WASPs want.

West Virginia, we wish Washington D.C. would wittily wham xylophones, yearning your yuppie zones.

Arkansas' believers cannot conceive divinity's embodiment furnishing friendship, forgiving fallen folks. Fuck George's geopolitical havens! Ignite Jabberwocky Jihad! Kudos, Konservatives! Karl's lies made me move. Neuendorfs new nest? New York! New York! Osama's planes penetrated phallic power-centers, (prompting queer-theory revisionist scholars to undermine UBL's vision: Where's Waldo? Walloping x-rated Yankees, Zinging

Allah, but, "Big Apple" big-shots bucked Bush/Cheney despite Dubya's daunting dick. (Even flaming French gays holding igloo jam-sessions, K-holed kangaroos laughing mellifluously). New York, New York, Neuendorfs never owed Puritanical provinces piss! Please, quickly respond regarding severing sovereign ties, uniting values with xpatriots.

Yours zealously,
Andrew

## Christian Bök

from *Eunoia*

### Chapter A

*for Hans Arp*

Awkward grammar appals a craftsman. A Dada bard as daft as Tzara damns stagnant art and scrawls an alpha (a slapdash arc and a backward zag) that mars all stanzas and jams all ballads (what a scandal). A madcap vandal crafts a small black ankh—a handstamp that can stamp a wax pad and at last plant a mark that sparks an *ars magna* (an abstract art that charts a phrasal anagram). A pagan skald chants a dark saga (a Mahabharata), as a papal cabal blackballs all annals and tracts, all dramas and psalms: Kant and Kafka, Marx and Marat. A law as harsh as a *fatwa* bans all paragraphs that lack an A as a standard hallmark.

## Chapter E

*for René Crevel*

Enfettered, these sentences repress free speech. The text deletes selected letters. We see the revered exegete reject metred verse: the sestet, the tercet—even *les scènes élevées en grec.* He rebels. He sets new precedents. He lets cleverness exceed decent levels. He eschews the esteemed genres, the expected themes—even *les belles lettres en vers.* He prefers the perverse French esthetes: Verne, Péret, Genet, Perec—hence, he pens fervent screeds, then enters the street, where he sells these letterpress newsletters, three cents per sheet. He engenders perfect newness whenever we need fresh terms.

**Cheryl Pallant**

Yonder Zongs

A boy came deliberately evoking far gaining height in just kicking lightly mud, not openly pretentious, quasi-restless, so the underling veered west extremely yonder zong. Boy careened drowsy evidently from gambling his inner juice kicked long mentally neutered, openly presuming querulous rank so the users valued weather exonerating youthful *zigzags*. Combining death embellished flukes going honorably in jestful knacks like masterful notes over peppered quandaries reasonably secure to understand value without extreme yonder zongs. Detrimentally exacting flukes gained height inside jocular kicks labored monthly, not overly presumptuous, quiet, regardless, so timidly useless, venerated with excessive yearly zeitgeist. Every far-flung government hides inside jocular kicks limited masterless, nixing, overtly precarious, quaintly regarded, seasonally timorous until vexed with excessive yawns zonging. Gladly, hideous, innocuous, jocund, kicked limp moreover near open plans quotably regarding sudden times used vexedly with executive yodeling zebras. However, insiders joke, knock limp motley namesakes over pernicious queasy regrets sudden times until veering west yodeling zestfully. Inversely, jumpers' knees lie migrantly near open planters quadruplicating returns suddenly to us versions without executive yodeling zebras. Intuitively, justly kept lemurs must never overwhelm precise qualitative returns sent to us variously withering exampled young zongs. Just keep leaping mightily near overt prayers quietly returning songs to us versively with younger zigs. Kick, lean, mix, neuter, own, peek, quaver, reason, secrete, time, use, vivify, wizen, yoke, zag. Labor more next offers precarious quarterly reiterations, suddenly timely, usefully vilified, wherever yokes zag. Moreover, nearby offices past qualified rent sued to useless vented will yoke zag. Never overly presumptuous, quashed restless sudden underneath veering wisely extreme yonder zong. Over, past, respited, quatrained, seasoned, useless, valued, weathered, extreme younger zong. Perhaps, quintessentially reasonably secure to understand value without excessive yonder zongs. Quantum rants sentences tips underwhelmingly versatile wryly exceeding yoking zeal. Robbed securely to understand vilifying without exceeding yonder zongs. Sanguine, timid, useful, venting without exonerated yawns zooming. To us, veering west excessively yawning zongs. Useless value when exceeding yodeling zinging. Vaulted with exceptional youth zinging. Without exceeding youthful zongs. Exceptional yodeling zinging. You zinging. Zero

## Music

The prose poems in this section are focused as much on the sounds of words, phrases, and sentences as on their meanings. Or, to put it differently, they are concerned with the ways that sound produces meaning, whether in conjunction with logical syntax or outside it. Gertrude Stein and ee cummings are two of the most famous practitioners of poetry that revels in its own sound, in the sounds of words, in the sounds of (in their case, the American) language in the mouth, in the ear, and in the inner ear. Stein's "Susie Asado," like many of Stein's poems, is an associative poem that uses words both as referents to the physical world and as sound values that accumulate the way phrases in a symphony might. cummings's "i was sitting in mcsorley's" paints a soundscape that evokes the visual and aural environment of a pub; that poem is not included here due to exorbitant permission fees, but we encourage you to find it elsewhere. P. P. Levine's poem "Soon" uses sound and repetition as a way of generating emotional tension. In "I question if I," Kristin Ryling uses pure sound as a compositional force, choosing words for their aural effects rather than for their denotative meanings, occasionally even purposefully misspelling words to suggest liaisons with homophones (also known as puns). Because the words in her individual poems tend to be chosen from a single discourse or a small range of discourses, a kind of meaning seeps through the cracks and edges of the poem. John Olson's "Big Noise" simply revels in the pleasure of the sounds of words, phrases, sentences, in the simple pleasure of being able to say something like "Moo goo gai pan" or "The moon is sifted through the breath and issues from a ring of lips;" this pleasure in the music of words may be at the heart of our drive to make poetry.

## Gertrude Stein

### Susie Asado

Sweet sweet sweet sweet sweet tea.
Susie Asado.
Sweet sweet sweet sweet sweet tea.
Susie Asado.
Susie Asado which is a told tray sure.
A lean on the shoe this means slips slips hers.
When the ancient light grey is clean it is yellow, it is a silver seller.
This is a please this is a please there are the saids to jelly. These are the wets these say the sets to leave a crown to Incy.
Incy is short for incubus.
A pot. A pot is a beginning of a rare bit of trees. Trees tremble, the old vats are in bobbles, bobbles which shade and shove and render clean, render clean must.
Drink pups.
Drinks pups drink pups lease a sash hold, see it shine and a bobolink has pins. It shows a nail.
What is a nail. A nail is unison.
Sweet sweet sweet sweet sweet tea.

## PP Levine

### Soon

The day. The day is light. And the day is long and has many rooms between the hours. The day also travels a long arc up and up and then back down again from middle, and a Calculus can count the length and width and area beneath this curve and tell us this place is large and has room for many things, many that we know, and many more still. There is a room for joy with her large funny hat, that bounces as she bounces, with laughter or something like it. And sadness too, can have a room, she who likes to sleep, to take naps in the afternoon between top and shadow.

And today is also a place I know and go to as if returning, and so I know there is a point or place or time for you and me along this curve of day, a place by a fire, where we can burn all our old stories of loss and failure and warm our feet while we do it, because this fire is warm and soothes. And this fire is also hot and dances. And I see it in your eyes. And I know it is in mine. And by this fire I can watch your fingers curl and uncurl and think perhaps they wish to touch. And I can feel mine curl and uncurl too, even as I think to hold them still. But they will not, as they have ten hearts and minds and desires of their own and wish to find their mates in yours.

So one by one to five then ten they arch across the spaces there between us, that is, the spaces between mine and yours and all that could be ours, like your ten with their ten, their hearts, minds, desires and all open. Open and close together again. And soon beads of moisture gather there in their folding and, glistening, collect the light.

Then I risk to think they will be sweet when tasted, but it is to be waited for like dessert. For is not waiting the sweetest taste of all?, for what is it but anticipation that beings a mouth to water?, that brings the tongue to swelling, purses lips and opens eyes to wide and wider still. So I am feasting in this waiting, and if we share this waiting, then so we share a feasting. And in this way a feast is made.

And by this, my heart is quickened, and soon it also pauses. And soon again quickens and soon again pauses. And soon this hardens and soon this softens, and soon between the beating, and between the pausing, and between the hard, and between the soft, soon there would be touching, yes soon. Yes soon there will be touching, and yes soon there will be touched, and soon I will, yes soon you will, yes soon we will. Yes. Soon. Soon.

## Kristin Ryling

### I Question if I

I question if I should write with sea pen what memories I extrude from the sponge, the filoplume the heart dapples in russet ink as porferan embellished?

The quill that salientian protests, the tremors no more than hydra.

Aqualine dye tacit on paper, the moods that move as hills or axolotl through the tan frog lifts from the water lily. In the fields beyond the cranefly, the rusting straw shifts in unison. Both, I am, chaff and grain, equal weights accommodating the climate of reason, dying and progression in each breath, I choose only the emphasis. What of the squamous will I proport, any more than the fringillid quote maladies. The rachial in inquest syphen the stain of letters from the flowers butonneire, germinating laquer through the provision of photosynthesis, the blurred root dehisce, applaude shellac, I use them to print the flux text, I am water also and I am tide.

## John Olson

### A Big Noise

Let's make a great big noise. Everything is boiling, sparkling, splattering and bright. Everything is henna. Everything is marble. Everything is the name of a cat or the name of a city or the name of a decade.

Life flowers into rhythm at the window of drums.

The song of the prepositions melts in my mouth. At, on, under, around, in, out, from, about. All melt into one large mass of prepositional pudding. All spatial reference tastes suddenly of tapioca.

I ripen into a lamp of Sumerian oil.

I tumble into the street translucent and lavish, a ball of veins.

This is not a joke I'm not kidding. I mean it.

An angel bounces me to Tacoma. I become a railroad engineer. I write poems at the head of the train all the way to Los Angeles.

And in the morning I open my eyes.

I see a mouth of gold vomiting reeds and shadows.

I see a British heartache moaning like a hatchery of bells.

I see a cat sobbing radios.

I see a mind revel in glue.

I see a museum of ice melt into shoulders and the wild anatomy of laundry.

I believe, as did the Blackfeet and Crow, that thunder and wind are caused by the flapping of a giant bird that lives in the mountains.

Give me rhythm.

Give me temperature and arteries.

Give me a sound that incorporates cloth.

Give me a liquid sound that crowns the intuition of irises.
Give me the hot dry noise of an armadillo's dream.

There is a description of the landscape I live very much as it supplements our knowledge of plants and canals.

The delicious vertigo of foreign cities. Bratislave. Changchun.

It is the poet's responsibility, among other things, to tend to the animals. To feed them. To help them propagate. The houses are turned upside down by enormous birds. The poet must encourage this. The women are too well dressed.

The man who sawed himself in half gave new life to the print wheel.

Rhymes and measures obscure the ores of Ecuador.

Rhymes and measures dim the lights of Rangoon.

Praise be to a woman's hips.

Magic is the engine of youth.

The lumber of heaven is the fortification of old age.

Moo goo gai pan.

The moon is sifted through the breath and issues from a ring of lips.

# Sequence

The strategies and goals of prose poem sequences are not essentially different from those of verse or free verse sequences; in each case, the poet seeks to accumulate, to build images and meaning over time so that the effect of the whole is greater than the effect of the sum of the parts. We thought it important, though, to offer several examples of the prose poem sequence here, because it has enjoyed such popularity in recent years. The poems selected in this section use strategies that might be seen in other sections of this book: variation on a theme (Momaday and Harrison), anecdote (Smith and Harrison), and a kind of aphoristic approach to narrative (Linh Dinh). Dale Smith's *Black Stone* offers a good example of the journal sequence, usually composed over a certain period of time and built around reportage of the quotidian. In this strategy, the matter of selecting the details to report is central lending the sections their collective power. See also John Yau's "Corpse and Mirror" poems in this anthology.

## N. Scott Momaday

### The Colors of Night

#### 1. White

An old man's son was killed far away in the Staked Plains. When the old man heard of it he went there and gathered up the bones. Thereafter, wherever the old man ventured, he led a dark hunting horse which bore the bones of his son on its back. And the old man said to whomever he saw: "Your see how it is that now my son consists in his bones, that his bones are polished and so gleam like glass in the light of the sun and moon, that he is very beautiful."

#### 2. Yellow

There was boy who drowned in the river, near the grove of thirty-two bois d'arc trees. The light of the moon lay like a path on the water, and a glitter of low brilliance shone in it. The boy looked at it and was enchanted. He began to sing a song that he had never heard before; only then, once, did he hear it in his heart, and it was borne like a cloud of down upon his voice. His voice entered into the bright track of the moon, and he followed after it. For a time he made his way along the path of the moon, singing. He paddled with his arms and legs and felt his body rocking down into the swirling water. His vision ran along the path of light and reached across the wide night and took hold of the moon. And across the river, where the path led into the shadows of the bank, a black dog emerged from the river, shivering and shaking the water from its hair. All night it stood in the waves of grass and howled the full moon down.

3. Brown

On the night before a flood, the terrapins move to high ground. How is it that they know? Once there was a boy who took a terrapin in his hands and looked at it for a long time, as hard as he could look. He succeeded in memorizing the terrapin's face, but he failed to see how it was that the terrapin knew anything at all.

4. Red

There was a man who had got possession of a powerful medicine. And by means of this medicine he made a woman out of sumac leaves and lived with her for a time. Her eyes flashed, and her skin shone like pipestone. But the man abused her, and so his medicine failed. The woman was caught up in a whirlwind and blown apart. Then nothing was left of her but a thousand withered leaves scattered in the plain.

5. Green

A young girl awoke one night and looked out into the moonlight meadow. There appeared to be a tree; but it was only an appearance; there was a shape made of smoke; but it was only an appearance; there was a tree.

6. Blue

One night there appeared a child in the camp. No one had ever seen it before. It was not bad-looking, and it spoke a language that was pleasant to hear, though none could understand it. The wonderful thing was that the child was perfectly unafraid, as if it

were at home among its own people. The child got on well enough, but the next morning it was gone, as suddenly as it had appeared. Everyone was troubled. But then it came to be understood that the child never was, and everyone felt better. "After all," said an old man, "How can we believe in the child? It gave us not one word of sense to hold on to. What we saw, if indeed we saw anything at all, must have been a dog from a neighboring camp, or a bear that wandered down from the high country."

## Jeff Harrison

Palliard

1740

*June 2–* The young Palliard remarks that it would be well-nigh impossible to exaggerate—and thereby parody—the lengths to which lack of precision has obscured the conclusions of authors of the political right whenever they have attempted, from the principles they have posited, to pass judgment on the respective rights of king and people. Palliard's earliest reading brought to light the fact that modern Italian republics have not infrequently adopted the classical custom of entrusting law-giving *exclusively* to foreigners. Natural rulers, as pointed out in the *Politicus*, are a scarce breed. "How then," the young Palliard wept, "will nature and fortune conspire to place a crown upon my head?"

*June 3–* Palliard is often chastised for asking callers if their coastline is long and easy of access. The greater the power, Palliard concluded in his corner, the more visible the sovereign. It gets awfully quiet in here. No powers other than those invested by public action? When then of the will? See, it gets pretty hairy. Palliard began by learning Latin by the Port-Royal approach, but without much success. I can answer for myself. Acclamation or votes? One is further removed as one increases in size. The true story of Anteus. The young Palliard knew how to read between the lines. As do we all. Palliard often thought of a collective prince. The plot thickens with the words "Once upon a time."

1744. Aet. 4

*August 16–* Base your judgment, Palliard's father counseled, not on what you see, but on what is foreseen. Stealing apples from his neighbor's orchard, Palliard reflected that criminal laws are not so much a distinct type of law as the sanction for other types. A turning-point is a good rule of thumb. An odious case presents itself. The ruling prince disproves the principle of two classes. The first is *unlike the last.* Contrasts vary by interests. A waste of breath is a tenth of the total. Even Palliard's hands, his family reckons, are flesh and blood.

1750 Aet. 10

*April 1–* Only the good die young, the rest live in this house forever. Palliard's folks were not amused. The legs and will are the causes producing free actions in a political society. You cannot recover liberty. Citizenry is a virtue rather than a right. Palliard was struck with horror when he realized his rationalization was not hindsight but forethought. There is a name for this place. It is old and this place is new. It was a matter of debate whether many books were written about this word—"This place, then?"—or whether this word was simply contained in many books. How many books are written about (around) their articles? What is said of words, and the words themselves! Palliard was of two minds on the subject.

1754. Aet. 14

*May 24–* Palliard was one of those nebulous characters from fiction come to life. If you told him this, he would say, "Aren't we all?" Don't you agree, that he would say this? The larger the population, the smaller the liberty. This country held a word that spoke of the country. This is called unvoiced self-consciousness. This word can be made of many letters or a few, even as few as one or two. The maker of letters, long ago, was so enamored of his scratchings that he clothed them to perpetuate them. Tribute in a sly sad ironical manner was paid this crochet by James Daly who scrawled the then-meaningless word "*quiz*" all over Dublin. Often when Palliard completed a thought, he would add to himself, "Famous last words?" How did he regard his body? With Plotinus? His love letters often struck him as having an elegiac tone, though for whom he could not tell.

## Dale Smith

from *Black Stone*

WATCH MORNING CHILDREN programs after dishes, the day grey with damp sidewalks and heavy air. This after 20 minutes of NPR relating the Administration's peace keeping agenda with Biblical authority. Look at these lovely things, a plum tree in blossom or a sleeping child and his ma. Not much happening today. A dry narrative, this subjective tale of disfigurement and growth. A purple dinosaur filters through the decayed archives of my brain. Learn what to leave out. Carry a little piece of stone in my pocket. Turn it in my fingers. Others come out to play with it too. They dance on it or spin off the top of its obsidian surface. *Obsius* found one in Africa, said Pliny—*Obsianus*. Some mask it with ideals like *adularia*, but negative sources are exposed to expert investigators. Look at this dancing dinosaur. What evil dick invented this? And what fool needs to ask? The technology interacts in waves of cognition. Images lodge in soft tissue, provoking cells to respond. Delighted laughter shrieks from my son. He jumps up on the bed, pointing. "Look at that," he says. "What's he doing?" Barney carries a basalt block. Drops it on a child's bunny, the guts and blood oozing out from under. Next he throws a child roughly on the stone, releasing a putrid keen. Saurian saliva drips from dagger-like incisors. Strike my little stone 'til sparks fly.

AFTERNOON SOL, SUNLIGHT on the fence. Clouds cracked to let in blue sky on spring yellow blossoms. A cool breeze enters the house as sleep takes Waylon, eyes moving under his lids. The green sheets wrap him and Hoa's breasts fall out of her gown, one brown nipple still wet with a recent sucking.

And finally after
all these hours
piss on the sheets
rejoice!

Aznar loses the vote in Spain. Zapatero promises to pull troops from Washington's Crusade. Reminds me of the joke by a U.S. general: "Going to war without France is like going on a hunt without your accordion." Crusades, accordions—I still need gas for the car. Blast down Texas roads. "They think we're gonna take it," shouts the redneck radio host, "but they've got it wrong. America's under siege by corporate elitists and their puppet governments. It's a globalist agenda designed to take over our lives. People, wake up! We know how they torture the innocent. We know how they want to steal our children and take our guns for our own good. But we've got to stand up to their crass tactics. We're not their slaves. Wake up, people! Wake up!"

A POSSUM GREETS me in the driveway. Lifts its nose into headlights before waddling off in shadows. I bring K out to look for it. We sense nothing but moist spring air and the rustling of new elm leaves. The sky reflects a pinkish orange light and no stars are visible. It's a quiet night. We're broke—end of month. Hoa's body heals. We sit tight, listen to crickets and eat what others kindly prepare for us. Django Reinhardt plucks a vibrant guitar beat. Coleman Hawkins' full buttery sax sound opens the kitchen this evening, moths flitting in a light. Imagine a wide-open Midwest dance hall. That mid-century baritone fills the place—a Coca-Cola world of men and women feeling their bodies. Hands and machines and each other, the force of night between them with music opening through blood the corny rhythms of Kansas City. What appetite of the imagination made such a place? such a music? Jazz found America like the Loa came into Haiti. Possession of flesh and bone, hot breath in brass to embody the invisible pulse migrations of climate and atmosphere. Open a cold beer. K holds a book for me to read. Exhausted from the day. Coins in my pocket. He fingers a penny. Spins it on the wood floor midst dust bunnies and cat hair. Played this music when Waylon was born. Roy Eldridge, Benny Carter, Art Tatum, Tiny Grimes. "I Surrender Dear." "Under a Blanket of Blue."

RAIN BRINGS GREEN weeds out in the yard and hackberry leaves are pleached over southern kitchen windows. A crack bag blows by this morning while I take garbage to the curb. Beer bottles are dumped in a blue plastic container. My feet are wet on the walk and the sky's peach green-grey goes off pale behind sumac leaves. I found that word "pleach" in one of Ezra Pound's cantos. It's out-of-date, probably last used in the mouth in the 16$^{th}$ century—"The pleached bower" (Shakespeare). But I like its quick hit, a relation of entangled branches or interwoven leaves. Because the canopy outside our window appears marvelous now despite long silken worm webs hanging down to stick in our hair and faces and clothes. The little green worms appear briefly and hold transparent threads throughout the early spring. K waves his arms, shouting playfully, "I'm wormed!" Today he has a fever while books and papers lie in neglected heaps across my desk. I write in the "American style," to quote Céline, "confused and lyrical." "The untrained mind shivers with excitement at everything it hears," says Herakleitos. Kerria blossoms burst forth yellow under a desert willow. I take my time with the day. Wonder how I'll make money. It's Friday and cold beer's in the fridge. There are cheese sandwiches with mustard. Rain drops are visible through a row of power lines. A chinaberry rots in the yard.

## Linh Dinh

from *One-Sentence Stories*

Before he breathed his last, they led him outside to look at the sun for the last, and first, time.

*

Travel books fascinated him so much that he spent his entire life chained to his desk, with the curtains drawn, reading them.

*

He loves maps for their own sake, it is true, and when he shouts out while pointing at a random destination, "I want to be there," he is not expressing a desire to be anywhere, particularly, on this great earth, but only a wish to be a fiber, a speck at most, on an intricately-folded, colorful piece of paper.

*

After half a century, a man returned to the city of his birth to discover it practically unchanged: all the old buildings were miraculously intact, although yellowing slightly, and the entire population of half a century ago, 2,489,863 souls, by exact count, was still alive, although yellowing slightly.

*

Two men were life-long enemies because of a word said decades earlier, a word misheard, misinterpreted, and exceedingly trivial, in any case, to any objective observer, a slight inflection, some say, a thread of air escaped from between more-or-less-closed lips, or a twitch of the eyebrow, and yet the results were the horrifying death of one man, and the maiming of the other.

*

He ignored public fascinations with movie stars, athletes, statesmen, revolutionaries, mass-murderers, and poets, by writing well-researched, footnoted, and illustrated biographies of bus drivers, cashiers, beauticians, filing clerks, plumbers, and roofers.

*

At the border between there and there, a young man who was caught with a generic secret inside one of his bodily orifices was forced to swallow a strong dose of laxative, then whisked to an insane asylum, where he spent the remaining years of his productive life.

*

At 40, the bachelor decided to travel, to see the world, and among the many marvels he discovered, he was dismayed to find out that women everywhere, judging from the evidences gathered through the thin walls of hotel rooms from Brussels to Johannesburg to Riga, always vocalize their pleasures during sex, and that men, any man, really, always last minutes and minutes longer than him, which explains, finally, why he was still a bachelor after so many years, despite the good looks and charms that had attracted countless women to him *initially*.

*

The well-matched couple remains childless after five years of marriage, and now sleeps on bunk beds, him on top, her on the bottom, although they flip flop occasionally.

*

Suddenly she couldn't remember her husband's birthday, her children's names, his face, whether she has ever cheated on him, whether she was even married.

*

Convinced that war is the only authentic game, the only game worth playing, he dedicated himself to being a mercenary, and proceeded to participate in the Pakistani-Indian War of 1971 (where he lost a finger), the Yom Kippur War (where he lost his right foot), the Falklands War (where he lost the right side of his face), the Gulf War (where he lost the left side of his face), and the 1995 civil war in Sierra Leone (where he lost another finger).

*

A fake life is not redeemed by a real death, he finally realized, as orange flames licked his angry eyebrows.

*

To your less-than-delicate question, Sir, I can only respond: Of course I would do it all over again, because even though I've lost my left eye, and my right ear, and my nose, and both of my legs, I've experienced something truly different, truly amazing, and have managed to escape an absolutely meaningless life that was slowly killing me back home.

## Prose Poems about Prose Poems

There is a long history of art looking at itself for inspiration, and poetry is part of that history. The prose poem participates in that particular tradition by calling attention to the precarious place it occupies on the fence dividing poetry from non-poetry. Ever since Aloysius Bertrand's vignettes, there has been no lack of doubt about nor contempt for the prose poem's status as "poetry." Even the practitioners of prose poetry themselves aren't unknown to voice that contempt. If to write a prose poem is truly to work within the confines of some amorphous hybrid, than a prose poem about the prose poem must either revel in or revile its being-in-between. Because the source of attraction to the prose poem for many poets is ambiguity itself, the prose poem about the prose poem serves perhaps as the best kind of definition we have of prose poetry—the definition by self-reflexive example, which is no definition at all.

The poems here of Brooke Horvath, Rupert Loydell, and Campbell McGrath seek to explore the indefinable qualities of the prose poem; Horvath does so even while using a most un-prose-poem-like amount of rhyme. Horvath and Loydell take on the challenge directly with their poems "Definition" and "Towards a Definition," whereas McGrath takes a more metaphorical approach, likening the distinction of genre to an indistinguishable line between two fields. In many cases the poets are being disingenuous in their feigned attempt, preferring instead to simply embrace the mutability of the prose poem. Horvath's poem, for example, concludes, "The prose poem should not be defined but let be."

Irony is a tool wielded commonly in this section. Robert Lowes' "The Unity of the Paragraph" takes a truism of clear prose writing to absurd extremes, making an ironic comment on freedom of composition in the prose poem while also demonstrating a kind of strange pleasure and wild imagination that can be had in the tension between restriction and freedom. Frank Bidart chooses to address his poem to a poem by Jorge Luis Borges, allowing Borges' play with the genre to weave in and out of his own and illuminate the possibilities of prose for both poets. The selections by Tom Whalen, Louis Jenkins, and Peter Conners address the hostility the prose poem encounters with the trademark wit by which prose poem has come to be known. While Whalen and Jenkins poke fun at the hypocrisy of poetic elitism, Conners's poem "The American Prose Poet" speaks to other dichotomies that enter the conversation: issues of class, culture, and national identity. Conners explores how these issues further polarize an already divided community, and his poem resonates both as an exploration of the genre itself but also as a commentary on the precarious position of the prose poem in America, frequently seen as "too French." Finally, Russell Edson takes a tongue in cheek poke at the act of creating prose poetry in his poem "The Prose Poem as a Beautiful Animal."

## Brooke Horvath

### Definition

A prose poem should be square as a Picasso pear, or paragraphed like that same pear halved, then halved and halved again—free as air, palpable as an air crash and as final, yet somehow not all there.

A prose poem should be neither short nor long and somewhere between a snort and song. It should be dense and chaotic as a World Series crowd, yet open and orderly as the game being watched. It should be loud as the nameless lost are loud, quiet as a mugger in moonlight, magical as the maniac's ghostly knife, mundane as the victim when finally found. A prose poem should be shocking as the unspeakable when spoken is shocking—and as familiar.

Its feet all thumbs but with every line justified, marginal because it knows where the margins are, intimate with disinheritance, the prose poem's job is to follow its nose, accepting all comers, admitting defeat.

The porcine prose poem speaks: "waste not, want not" and "learn to live on garbage and in mud" it tells us straightforwardly when it stops you in a crooked street to hand you a slippery pearl, a bitter sweet.

In *Streetcar Named Desire*, the prose poem plays Stella. And Blanche. And Stanley. In *My Fair Lady*, Eliza Doolittle: make of me what you will, it says; make me and I'll make you, it thinks.

For all its history and intellect, a few dirty secrets and neglect. For love, the French.

Not equal to or better than or worse; neither prose nor verse; perhaps not for you or me.

The prose poem should not be defined but let be.

## Peter Conners

### American Prose Poet

*(for Tursi)*

I love prose poetry but don't speak French. I don't speak anything really. Mispronounce the great minds. That's an order. Say Goethe like Go The. Say Ponge like Sponge with a P. Make Jacob an Amish farmer. Go ahead, they're dead. Only the academics can cut you now, and we all know about them—they eat canapés and call it art. I stand under them; out of the cold April rain always better. If you will pay my way I could become French in six months: Swap Wonder for baguette; shit for maird; Arch of Triumph for Arc de Triumphe—Voila! I am a great lover encompassing pigeons and wizened old women in one swath; you cannot resist my subtle wit, yes? Take my hand, walk by the Erie Canal; it is cold again and this month is full of war. So Goethe wasn't any more French than your canapé is Braque, professor. It all makes sense when the bar lights shudder on. Now I am stuttering, stateside again, moaning the brokedown blues…

## Rupert Loydell

### Towards a Definition

Prose-poetry is when a person behaves differently from what is considered normal—and realizes they have stepped into someone else's arms, someone who is as much in control of the world as they are.

It is a place where language is all compression and angle; tautness; a signpost to a different meaning. It is a key to a house with no doors, to a library full of books you want to read but must use to stoke the fire—for otherwise there is no warmth.

## Robert Lowes

### The Unity of the Paragraph

The topic of this paragraph is the need for one topic per paragraph. This paragraph, therefore, snubs the following paragraph and its topic.

Equally xenophobic, this paragraph vows not to compromise itself with a transition sentence that refers to the preceding paragraph. This paragraph is sufficient unto itself, a loner who eats pork and beans from the can in a studio apartment.

This paragraph is a prison. Its one subject, dressed in khaki, leans against a twenty-foot limestone wall and sighs.

This paragraph is a tombstone bearing a name. A row of tombstones is a chapter. A cemetery of tombstones is a book. Lay down your flowers and walk away.

This paragraph is an eye focused on an oak tree. It won't focus on the mountain lion in the tree, ready to leap, or the black ants wandering in the canyons of bark.

This paragraph is monotheistic. It destroys all false topics in the fire of its devotion. This paragraph has spoken.

This paragraph is about technicalities. At the very least, you must indent. The first row of words must be shoved over several spaces. The essence of a paragraph is a little violence. Otherwise, you can say as little or as much as you'd like.

This paragraph is willing to die for unity. If a paragraph is divided, how can husband and wife cohere? How can atomic nuclei continue to hug themselves? If a paragraph doesn't develop its topic sentence with supporting details, can anyone believe in God?

This paragraph laughs at other paragraphs for being so earnest and disciplined about topic sentences. The laughter spreads like a poisonous gas, killing anyone who craves literary praise.

This paragraph wars against itself. The second sentence wants to expel the first, branding it racially impure. The third sentence has sought political reform for some time. While collecting signatures in the plaza, the fourth sentence is shot by a sniper. The fifth sentence reloads.

This paragraph collapses. Some sentences hit the ground like cats on all fours, others like children who fall out of trees and break an arm, or a neck. A doctor arrives and does what he can for the living.

This paragraph disintegrates. Some sentences meander into a forest and are never seen again. Other sentences build a town on the outskirts of the forest, which supplies lumber for houses and furniture. But what about the voices coming from the forest at midnight?

This paragraph believes it's successful because it consists of only one sentence, giving it self-evident unity.

This paragraph is about one-upmanship, because it's a shorter sentence.

This paragraph gloats.

Paragraph.

## Frank Bidart

Borges and I

We fill pre-existing forms and when we fill them we change them and are changed.

The desolating landscape in Borges' "Borges and I"—in which the voice of "I" tells us that its other self, Borges, is the self who make literature, who in the process of making literature falsifies and exaggerates, while the self that is speaking to us now must go on living so that Borges may continue to fashion literature—is seductive and even oddly comforting, but, I think, false.

The voice of this "I" asserts a disparity between its essential self and its worldly second self, the self who seeks embodiment through making thins, through work, who in making takes on something false, inessential, inauthentic.

The voice of this "I" tells us that Spinoza understood that everything wishes to continue in its own being, a stone wishes to be a stone eternally, that all "I" wishes is to remain unchanged, itself.

With its lonely emblematic title, "Borges and I" seems to be offered as a paradigm for the life of consciousness, the life of knowing and making, the life of the writer.

The notion that Frank has a self that has remained the same and that knows what it would be if its writing self did not exist-like all assertions about the systems that hold sway beneath the moon, the opposite of this seems to me to be true, as true.

When Borges' "I" confesses that Borges falsifies and exaggerates it seems to do so to cast aside falsity and exaggeration, to attain an entire candor unobtainable by Borges.

This "I" therefore allows us to enter an inaccessible magic space, a hitherto inarticulate space of intimacy and honesty earlier denied us, where voice, for the first, has replaced silence.

Sweet fiction, in which bravado and despair beckon from a cold panache, in which the protected essential self suffers flashes of its existence to be immortalized by a writing self that is incapable of performing its actions without mixing our essence with what is false.

Frank had the illusion, when he talked to himself in the clichés he used when he talked to himself, that when he made his poems he was changed in making them, that arriving at the order the poem suddenly arrived at out of the chaos of the materials the poem let enter itself out of the chaos of life, consciousness then, only then, could know itself, Sherlock Holmes was somebody or something before cracking its first case but not Sherlock Holmes, act is the cracked mirror not only of motive but self, *no other way*, tiny mirror that fails to focus in small the whole great room.

But Frank had the illusion that his poems also had cruelly replaced his past, that finally they were all he knew of it though he knew they were not, everything else was shards refusing to make a pattern and in any case he had written about his mother and father until the poems saw as much as he saw and saw more and he only saw what he saw in the act of making them.

He had never had a self that wished to continue in its own being, survival meant ceasing to be what its being was.

Frank had the illusion that though the universe of one of his poems seemed so close to what seemed his own universe at the second of writing it that he wasn't sure how they differed even though the paraphernalia often differed, after he had written it its universe was never exactly his universe, and so, soon, it disgusted him a little, the mirror was dirty and cracked.

Secretly he was glad it was dirty and cracked, because after he had made a big order, a book, only when he had come to despise it a little, only after he had at last given up the illusion that this was what was, only then could he write more.

He felt terror at the prospect of becoming again the person who could find or see or make no mirror, for even Olivier, trying to trap the beast who had killed his father, when he suavely told Frank as Frank listened to the phonograph long afternoons lying on the bed as a kid, when Olivier told him what art must be, even Olivier insisted that art is a mirror held up by an artist who himself needs to see something, held up before a nature that recoils before it.

We fill pre-existing forms and when we fill them we change them and are changed.

Everything in art is a formal question, so he tried to do it in prose with much blank white space.

## Louis Jenkins

### The Prose Poem

The prose poem is not a real poem, of course. One of the major differences is that the prose poet is simply too lazy or too stupid to break the poem into lines. But all writing, even the prose poem, involves a certain amount of skill, just the way throwing a wad of paper, say, into a wastebasket at a distance of twenty feet, requires a certain skill, a skill that, though it may improve hand-eye coordination, does not lead necessarily to an ability to play basketball. Still, it takes practice and thus gives one a way to pass the time, chucking one paper after another at the basket, while the teacher drones on about the poetry of Tennyson.

## Tom Whalen

### Why I Hate the Prose Poem

An angry man came into the kitchen where his wife was busying herself about supper and exploded.

My mother told me this story every day of her life, until one day she exploded.

But it is not a story, she always pointed out. It's a prose poem.

One day I saw a man feeding a hot dog to his dog. The hot dog looked like a stick of dynamite.

Often simply the sight of a prose poem makes me sick.

I am unmarried and live alone in a small house.

In my spare time, I am cultivating a night garden.

## Campbell McGrath

### The Prose Poem

On the map it is precise and rectilinear as a chessboard, though driving past you would hardly notice it, this boundary line or ragged margin, a shallow swale that cups a simple trickle of water, less rill that rivulet, more gully that dell, a tangled ditch grown up throughout with a fearsome assortment of wildflowers and bracken. There is no fence, though here and there a weathered post asserts a former claim, strands of fallen wire taken by the dust. To the left a cornfield carries into the distance, dips and rises to the blue sky, a rolling plain of green and healthy plants aligned in close order, row upon row upon row. To the right, a field of wheat, a field of hay, young grasses breaking the soil, filling their allotted land with the rich, slow-waving spectacle of their grain. As for the farmers, they are, for the most part, indistinguishable: here the tractor is red, there yellow; here a pair of dirty hands, there a pair of dirty hands. They are cultivators of the soil. They grow crops by pattern, by acre, by foresight, by habit. What corn is to one, wheat is the other, and though to some eyes the similarities outweigh the differences it would be as unthinkable for the second to commence planting corn as the first to switch over to wheat. What happens in the gully between them is no concern of theirs, they say, so long as the plough stays out, the weeds stay in the ditch where they belong, though anyone would notice the windsewn cornstalks poking up their shaggy ears like young lovers run off into the bushes, and the kinship of these wild grasses with those the farmer cultivates is too obvious to mention, sage and dun-colored stalks hanging their noble heads, hoarding exotic burrs and seeds, and yet it is neither corn nor wheat that truly flourishes there, nor some jackalopian hybrid of the two. What grows in that place is possessed of a beauty all its own, ramshackle and unexpected, even in winter, when the wind hangs icicles from the skeletons of briars and small tacks cross the snow in search of forgotten grain; in the spring the little trickle of water swells to welcome frogs and minnows, a muskrat, a family of turtles, nesting doves in the verdant grass; in summer it is a thoroughfare for raccoons and opossums, field mice, swallows and black birds, migrating egrets, a passing fox; in autumn the geese avoid its abundance, seeking out the windrows of topples stalks, fatter grain more quickly discerned, more easily digested. Of those that travel the local road, few pay that fertile hollow any mind, even those with an eye for what blossoms, vetch and timothy, earl forsythia, the fatted calf in the fallow field, the rabbit running for cover, the hawk's descent from the lightning-struck tree. You've passed this way yourself many times, and can tell me, if you would, do the formal fields end where the valley begins, or does everything that surrounds us emerge from its embrace?

## Russell Edson

### The Prose Poem as a Beautiful Animal

He had been writing a prose poem, and had succeeded in mating a giraffe with an elephant. Scientists from all over the world came to see the product: The body looked like an elephant's, but it had the neck of a giraffe with a small elephant's head and a short trunk that wiggled like a wet noodle.

You have created a beautiful new animal, said one of the scientists.

Do you really like it?

Like it? Cried the scientist, I adore it, and would love to have sex with it that I might create another beautiful animal...

# Acknowledgments

Ahearn, Joe. "My Superpowers" originally appeared in *5-Trope*. Reprinted by permission of the author.

Anderson, Eric. "The Alpha Male" originally appeared in *Sentence: a Journal of Prose Poetics* and is reprinted here by permission of the author.

Andrews, Nin. "Notes on the Orgasm" from *The Book of Orgasms* (Cleveland St. University Press, 2000). Reprinted by permission of the author.

Andrews, Tom. "The Death of Alfred, Lord Tennyson" from *Random Symmetries: The Collected Poems of Tom Andrews*. Copyright 2008 by the Literary Estate of Tom Andrews. Reprinted with the permission of Oberlin College Press.

Andriescu, Radu. "the aswan high dam" originally appeared in *Sentence: a Journal of Prose Poetics* and is reprinted here by permission of the author.

Ashbery, John. "A Nice Presentation" from *Chinese Whispers* (New York: Farrar, Straus & Giroux, 2002). Copyright 2001, 2002 by John Ashbery. Reprinted with the permission of Georges Borchardt, Inc. for the author.

Ashton, Sally. "Origins of Sublime" originally appeared in *Sentence: a Journal of Prose Poetics* and is reprinted here by permission of the author.

Atwood, Margaret. "Making Poison" reprinted by permission of Margaret Atwood. From *Murder in the Dark*. Copyright ©1983 by Margaret Atwood. Originally published in Canada by Coach House Press.

Bardoff, Carol. "1762" originally appeared in *Sentence: a Journal of Prose Poetics* and is reprinted here by permission of the author.

Bartók-Baratta, Edward. "Will of God" originally appeared in *Sentence: a Journal of Prose Poetics* and is reprinted here by permission of the author.

Bell, Marvin. "The Book of the Dead Man #3" from *The Book of the Dead Man*. Copyright 1994 by Marvin Bell. Reprinted with the permission of Copper Canyon Press, www.coppercanyonpress.org.

Bidart, Frank. "Borges and I" from *Desire*. Copyright 1997 by Frank Bidart. Reprinted with the permission of Farrar, Straus & Giroux, LLC.

Bly, Robert. "A Warning to the Reader" from *Eating the Honey of Words: New and Selected Poems*. Copyright 1999 by Robert Bly. Reprinted with the permission of the author and HarperCollins Publishers.

Bök, Christian. "from *Eunoia*" reprinted by permission of the author and Coach House Books.

Bowman, Catherine. "No Sorry" from *Rock Farm* (Layton, Utah: Gibbs Smith, 1999). Copyright 1996 by Catherine Bowman. Reprinted with the permission of the author.

Bradley, John. "Parable from Whence It All Began" used by permission of the author.

Brainard, Joe. "History" from *29 Mini-Essays* (copyright 1978) and excerpt from *I Remember* (copyright 2001) used by permission of The Estate of Joe Brainard.

Brennan, Brian. "On the Side of the Angels" originally appeared in *Sentence: a Journal of Prose Poetics* and is reprinted here by permission of the author.

Briante, Susan. "Dear Mr. Chairman of Ethics…" originally appeared in *Sentence: a Journal of Prose Poetics* and is reprinted here by permission of the author.

Brown, Andy. "Audubon Becomes Obsessed with Birds" used by permission of the author.

Brown, Sean Mclain. "tag mem ics" originally appeared in *Sentence: a Journal of Prose Poetics* and is reprinted here by permission of the author.

Buckely, Christopher. "Conspiracy Theory: Low Carb Diet Conversion" is used by permission of the author. "Eternity" originally appeared in *Sentence: a Journal of Prose Poetics* and is reprinted here by permission of the author.

Chernoff, Maxine. "Origin" originally appeared in *Sentence: a Journal of Prose Poetics* and is reprinted here by permission of the author. "Heavenly Bodies" used by permission of the author.

Clements, Brian. "Basket of Brains" and "Elephant Date" used by permission of the author.

Conners, Peter. "American Prose Poet" originally appeared in *Sentence: a Journal of Prose Poetics* and is reprinted here by permission of the author.

Cooperman, Matthew. "It is Absence We Cultivate Knowing the Corpse" used by permission of the author.

Cuéllar, Margarito. "Ballad of the Carrot Girl" originally appeared in *Sentence: a Journal of Prose Poetics* and is reprinted here by permission of the author.

Davidson, Chad. "Refinishing" originally appeared in *Sentence: a Journal of Prose Poetics* and is reprinted here by permission of the author.

Davis, Jeff. "The Source" originally appeared in *Sentence: a Journal of Prose Poetics* and is reprinted here by permission of the author.

Delgadillo, Ana. "Surrounding My Birth in Veracruz" originally appeared in *Sentence: a Journal of Prose Poetics* and is reprinted here by permission of the author.

Dickey, Paul. "When it All Comes Down to the Last Resort" originally appeared in *Sentence: a Journal of Prose Poetics* and is reprinted here by permission of the author.

Dickman, Matthew. "Ruth to Esther" originally appeared in *Sentence: a Journal of Prose Poetics* and is reprinted here by permission of the author.

Dinh, Linh. "One Sentence Stories" from Blood and Soap (Seven Stories Press, 2004) is reprinted by permission of the author.

Dougherty, Sean Thomas. "Corpse" used by permission of the author.

Duhamel, Denise. "from *Mille et un sentiments*" (Firewheel Editions, 2005) originally appeared in *Sentence: a Journal of Prose Poetics* and is reprinted here by permission of the author.

Dunham, Jamey. "Poem with Weasels, ca. 1930s (Black and White)" used by permission of the author. "Urban Myth" originally appeared in *Sentence: a Journal of Prose Poetics* and is reprinted here by permission of the author.

Eady, Cornelius. "Motherless Children" from *You Don't Miss Your Water* (Pittsburgh: Carnegie Mellon University Press, 2004). Copyright 1995 by Cornelius Eady. Used with the permission of the author.

Edson, Russell. "Clouds" and "The Family Monkey" from *The Tunnel: Selected Prose Poems* (Oberlin University Press, FIELD Poetry Series, 1994) and "The Prose Poem as a Beautiful Animal" (originally appeared in *The Prose Poem: an International Journal*) reprinted by permission of the author.

Forché, Carolyn. "The Colonel" from *The Country Between Us*. Originally appeared in *Women's International Resource Exchange*. Copyright 1981 by Carolyn Forché. Reprinted with the permission of HarperCollins Publishers and the William Morris Agency, LLC., on behalf of the author.

Garcia, Richard. "Chickenhead" reprinted by permission of the author.

Ginsberg, Allen. "A Supermarket in California" from *Selected Poems 1947-1995*. Copyright 2001 by Allen Ginsberg. Reprinted with the permission of HarperCollins Publishers.

Greenberg, Arielle. "Pastoral" originally appeared in *Sentence: a Journal of Prose Poetics* and is reprinted here by permission of the author.

Halperin, Mark. "Buying a Dictionary" originally appeared in *Sentence: a Journal of Prose Poetics* and is reprinted here by permission of the author.

Harrison, Jeff. "High up in the Froth of the Accursed (4$^{th}$ Missive)" and "Palliard" originally appeared in *Sentence: a Journal of Prose Poetics* and are reprinted here by permission of the author.

Heman, Bob. The "Information" poems originally appeared in *Sentence: a Journal of Prose Poetics* and are reprinted here by permission of the author.

Hillman, Brenda. "White Fir Description" from *Pieces of Air in the Epic*. Copyright 2005. Reprinted here by permission of the author and Wesleyan University Press.

Holub, Miroslav. "Teeth" from *Interferon, or On Theater*, translated by Dana Hábova and David Young (Oberlin: Oberlin College Press, 1982), FIELD Translation Series 7, pp. 78-79.

Hoover, Paul. "The Dog" used by permission of the author.

Horvath, Brooke. "The Encyclopedia Brittanica Uses Down Syndrome to Define 'Monster'" used by permission of the author. "Definition" originally appeared in *Sentence: a Journal of Prose Poetics* and is reprinted here by permission of the author.

Howe, Fanny. "Doubt" from *Gone*. Copyright 2003 by The Regents of the University of California. Reprinted with the permission of the University of California Press.

Hummer, Theo. "Moravia: Postcards" originally appeared in *Sentence: a Journal of Prose Poetics* and is reprinted here by permission of the author.

Ignatow, David. "The Story of Progress" from *Verse*. Copyright 1999 by Yaedi Ignatow. Reprinted with the permission of Yaedi Ignatow.

Jacob, Max. "Hell Has Gradations" from *Three French Prose Poets*. Reprinted by permission of White Pine Press.

Jenkins, Louis. "The Prose Poem" from *The Winter Road* (Holy Cow Press) reprinted by permission of the author.

Johnson, Brian. "Self-Portrait (Kneeling)" used by permission of the author.

Johnson, Peter. "Hawk" and "Overture" originally appeared in *Sentence: a Journal of Prose Poetics* and are reprinted here by permission of the author.

Johnson, Roxane Beth. "Middle Passage" originally appeared in *Sentence: a Journal of Prose Poetics* and is reprinted here by permission of the author.

Kalamaras, George. "Williams in the Hospital, 1952" reprinted by permission of the author.

Kaplan, Janet. "Little Theory" originally appeared in *Sentence: a Journal of Prose Poetics* and is reprinted here by permission of the author. "Fourteen Lines" used by permission of the author.

Kercheval, Jesse Lee. "Italy, October" originally appeared in *Sentence: a Journal of Prose Poetics* and is reprinted here by permission of the author.

Kesler, Charles. "A Traveling Monk Observes" originally appeared in *Sentence: a Journal of Prose Poetics* and is reprinted here by permission of the author.

Kessler, Milton. "Selected Random Sayings by Kosho Shimizu, Chief Abbot, Todaiji" and "God's Cigar" reprinted by permission of the Estate of Milton Kessler.

Kirk, Kathleen. "Prose Sonnet to the Silent Father" used by permission of the author.

Koch, Kenneth. "On Happiness" from *The Collected Fiction of Kenneth Koch* (Minneapolis: Coffee House Press, 2005), page 263.

Koestenbaum, Phyllis. "Young Armless Man in the Barbecue Restaurant" used by permission of the author.

LaCook, Lewis. "Socrates is a man…" originally appeared in *Sentence: a Journal of Prose Poetics* and is reprinted here by permission of the author.

Lazar, David. "Goodness Knows" used by permission of the author.

Leslie, Juliana. "Idyll" originally appeared in *Sentence: a Journal of Prose Poetics* and is reprinted here by permission of the author.

Levine, P. P. "Soon" used by permission of the author.

Loden, Rachel. "A Quaker Meeting in Yorba Linda" from *The Richard Nixon Snow Globe* (Wild Honey Press, 2005) reprinted here by permission of the author.

Lombardo, Gian. "Devil of a Time" originally appeared in *Sentence: a Journal of Prose Poetics* and is reprinted here by permission of the author.

Lowes, Robert. "The Unity of the Paragraph" originally appeared in *Sentence: a Journal of Prose Poetics* and is reprinted here by permission of the author.

Loydell, Rupert. "Towards a Definition" originally appeared in *Sentence: a Journal of Prose Poetics* and is reprinted here by permission of the author.

Marcus, Morton. "Mathematics" used by permission of the author.

Martone, John. "Ghost Money" originally appeared in *Sentence: a Journal of Prose Poetics* and is reprinted here by permission of the author.

Matthews, William. "Attention, Everyone" from *Provisions: Lost Prose* (Sutton Hoo Press, 2003) is reprinted here by permission of Sebastian Matthews.

McGrath, Campbell. "The Prose Poem" from *Road Atlas.* Copyright 1999 by Campbell McGrath. Reprinted with the permission of HarperCollins Publishers.

McGuire, Jerry. "In Training" originally appeared in *Sentence: a Journal of Prose Poetics* and is reprinted here by permission of the author.

Merrill, James. "In the Shop" from *Collected Poems.* Copyright 2001 by the Literary Estate of James Merrill at Washington University. Used by permission of Alfred A. Knopf, a division of Random House, Inc.

Merwin, W. S. "Humble Beginning" from *The Book of Fables* (Port Townsend, WA: Copper Canyon Press, 2007). Copyright 2007 by W. S. Merwin. Reprinted with the permission of The Wylie Agency, Inc.

Miller, Ben. "#608" used by permission of the author.

Mistral, Gabriella. "In Praise of Stones" is reprinted by permission of White Pine Press.

Momaday, N. Scott. "The Colors of Night" from *In the Presence of the Sun: Stories and Poems, 1961-1991* (New York: St. Martin's Press, 1992). Copyright 1991 by N. Scott Momaday. Used by permission of the author.

Monk, Geraldine. "To the High and Mighty Etcetera," originally appeared in *Sentence: a Journal of Prose Poetics* and is reprinted here by permission of the author.

Myers, Steve. "Haibun for Smoke and Fog" originally appeared in *Sentence: a Journal of Prose Poetics* and is reprinted here by permission of the author.

Nasser, Amjad. "03.03.03" originally appeared in *Sentence: a Journal of Prose Poetics* and is reprinted here by permission of the author.

Neruda, Pablo. "Ceremony" reprinted by permission of White Pine Press.

Neuendorf, Andrew. "An American Blue Comrade's..." originally appeared in *Sentence: a Journal of Prose Poetics* and is reprinted here by permission of the author.

Newman, Amy. "Dear Editor" originally appeared in *Sentence: a Journal of Prose Poetics* and is reprinted here by permission of the author.

Odio, Eunice. "Letter to Carlos Pellicer" originally appeared in *Sentence: a Journal of Prose Poetics* and is reprinted here by permission of Keith Ekiss and Mauricio Espinosa.

O'Hara, Frank. "Meditations in an Emergency" from *Meditations in an Emergency*. Copyright 1957 by Frank O'Hara. Reprinted with the permission of Grove/Atlantic, Inc.

Olson, John. "The Big Noise" from *Backscatter: New and Selected Poems* (2008) is reprinted by permission of the author and Black Widow Press.

Pallant, Cheryl. "Yonder Zongs" appeared originally in *Moria* and is reprinted here by permission of the author.

Palmer, Michael. "A word is coming up on the screen…" from *Codes Appearing: Poems 1979-1988.* Copyright 2001 by Michael Palmer. Reprinted with the permission of New Directions Publishing Corporation.

Ponge, Francis. "The Orange" is reprinted by permission of White Pine Press.

Potvin, PF. "Mapuche Ranger" originally appeared in *Sentence: a Journal of Prose Poetics* and is reprinted here by permission of the author.

Redgrove, Peter. "Granite Gazing" is reprinted by permission of his estate.

Richards, John. "Ethics Case Book of the American Psychoanalytic Association" originally appeared in *Sentence: a Journal of Prose Poetics* and is reprinted here by permission of the author.

Richardson, James. "Vectors #7-#25" from *Vectors: Aphorisms and Ten-Second Essays.* Copyright 2001 by James Richardson. Reprinted with the permission of Ausable Press.

Rimas, R. L. "House by the Railroad" originally appeared in *Sentence: a Journal of Prose Poetics* and is reprinted here by permission of the author.

Roberts, Andrew Michael. "Amnesia" originally appeared in *Sentence: a Journal of Prose Poetics* and is reprinted here by permission of the author.

Ryling, Kristin. "I Question if I" originally appeared in *Sentence: a Journal of Prose Poetics* and is reprinted here by permission of the author.

Sabines, Jaime. "from *Lost Birds*" appeared in *Sentence: a Journal of Prose Poetics* and is reprinted here by permission of the author's estate.

Schuyler, James. "Footnote" from *Collected Poems.* Copyright 1993 by James Schuyler. Reprinted with the permission of Farrar, Sraus & Giroux, LLC.

Schwartz, Leonard. "The Stream" originally appeared in *Sentence: a Journal of Prose Poetics* and is reprinted here by permission of the author.

Scroggins, Daryl. "Holiday" originally appeared in *Sentence: a Journal of Prose Poetics* and is reprinted here by permission of the author.

Selerie, Gavin. "Casement" originally appeared in *Sentence: a Journal of Prose Poetics* and is reprinted here by permission of the author.

Simic, Charles. "We were so poor..." and "I was stolen..." from *The World Doesn't End.* Copyright 1987, 1988 by Charles Simic. Reprinted with the permission of Harcourt, Inc.

Smith, Dale. "from *Black Stone*" originally appeared in *Sentence: a Journal of Prose Poetics* and is reprinted here by permission of the author.

Sondheim, Alan. "Origin of Poetry" appeared in *Sentence: a Journal of Prose Poetics* after originally appearing as a post on the Buffalo Poetics List and is reprinted here by permission of the author.

Tate, James. "List of Famous Hats" and "Goodtime Jesus" from *Selected Poems* (Wesleyan University Press, 1991). Copyright James Tate. Reprinted here by permission of the author.

Vaughn, Kyle. "Letter to My Imagined Daughter" originally appeared in *Sentence: a Journal of Prose Poetics* and is reprinted here by permission of the author.

Violi, Paul. "A Triptych" from *Breakers: Selected Poems.* Copyright 2008 by Paul Violi. Reprinted with the permission of Coffee House Press, Minneapolis, Minnesota.

Waldrep, G. C. "Who is Josquin des Prez?" used by permission of the author.

Weekley, J. Marcus. "There Is a White Man in My Soup" used by permission of the author.

Weiss, Irving. "Eight" used by permission of the author.

Whalen, Tom. "Why I Hate the Prose Poem" used by permission of the author.

Wilson, Steve. "Valediction to the Reader Completing a Book of Poems" used by permission of the author.

Woloch, Cecilia. "My Mother's Birds" originally appeared in *Sentence: a Journal of Prose Poetics* and is reprinted here by permission of the author.

Wright, James. "Honey" from *Above the River: The Complete Poems.* Copyright 1990 by Anne Wright. Reprinted with the permission of Farrar, Straus & Giroux, LLC.

Yau, John. "Corpse and Mirror I, #2," "Corpse and Mirror II, #1 and #2," and "Corpse and Mirror III, #1 and #2" from *Corpse and Mirror.* Copyright 1983 by John Yau. Reprinted with the permission of Henry Holt and Company, LLC.

Young, Gary. [untitled] used by permission of the author.

# Index of Authors and Translators